WHEN TO RUN, BORN SCARED

STEPHANIE KING

authorHOUSE®

AuthorHouse™
1663 Liberty Drive
Bloomington, IN 47403
www.authorhouse.com
Phone: 833-262-8899

Published by AuthorHouse 12/26/2020

ISBN: 978-1-6655-0682-3 (sc)
ISBN: 978-1-6655-0683-0 (e)

Print information available on the last page.

PREFACE

This book is about the survival, strength, and determination of a young girl born into a demonic family and how she successfully overcame the criminal abuse by the many evil monsters who hunted her. When many would have just given up, she fought back and refused to let them win.

PROLOGUE

Aside from genetics, we are all born the same: innocent virgins of life. It then remains the question of how we are raised from birth; the confidence we gain, the love and nurturing we need, the support and happiness we thrive on, the trust we must earn as we try to find our place in life, and the happy memories we can look back on and be grateful for. These in part define us in our goals of who we can work toward becoming and hopefully someday be. We were meant to learn, live, laugh, love, and flourish throughout childhood as we grow into successful adults we can be proud of.

Many overcome the usual obstacles growing up, but then there are the unfortunate few who are forced to learn horrific fear and do not understand that survival is even an option. When the horror and hell of a child's experience enters into the equation, it becomes complicated, and lives can take a traumatic turn for the worse. Instead of successful adults, they become victims of circumstances that lead them off into a different direction, never knowing that there are tools that could help them to fight against those evils, and win.

I didn't know that extreme pain and suffering was part of any learning curve, but my genetics proved to unveil a great strength and ability given to me that got me through each battle. It was a strength that grew when my sordid life led me onto the next battle, which was much worse than the last.

I chose to fight, but it came at an outrageous cost that nearly destroyed me. Somehow, it became a war I didn't understand and was not even prepared to fight. It wasn't long into my life when I realized that surviving was a viable option, that if I was totally committed to it, regardless of the perfidious horrors that unfolded along the way, I could actually stand a chance of winning. I accepted my life the way it was and learned way too young that I could fail if I didn't work hard enough to conquer the perils, or they could easily end my life in a moment's weakness.

We are all affected by influences from those around us, especially; our parents and siblings, whom we first learn from. Those lessons could easily ascend to lasting scars if we are not vigilant about attending to their extreme forces, leaving our future to the demons who could find us. For me, it was either adapt or be destroyed, so I persistently fought each fight, trying to focus on a future that was so far off in the distance that at times I questioned its existence. I lived my life day by day and did whatever I had to do to survive.

Without hope in life, we simply become shells of a body with a mind overpowered by others, and I refused to allow that to happen to me. It took time, but I did learn to become who I wanted to be, and I am proud to be the person I am today. I learned just how much more inner strength I could have if I somehow channeled my resentment into a positive existence, instead of succumbing to the monsters that had the ability to destroy me.

My childhood was filled with cruelty, hostility, and evil. Any attempt to object or try to fight their evil control ended in a punishment without my understanding why. I guess I missed that particular evil gene, which explains a lot about my life now and my willingness to keep fighting the injustices, with the determination to survive and succeed.

There was no legal help or protection for children back then, that I was aware of, nor was there any punishment severe enough for those horrific bastards hurting me, not like there is today. I was a very young child, alone to fight in a world I had no idea how to fight, but something inside of me knew I had to survive or die trying. I refused to give up, and my childhood is now a testament of the strength, courage, and success, that I have made for myself today, devoid of any further fears.

CHAPTER 1

Our father, Jean, was the oldest of five children. His family had emigrated from Europe when he was a lad too young to remember, but it was a time when immigrants were well received in Canada, fleeing from the terror of the war oversees. Of the five children, three of the male siblings would unfortunately be called to serve in the armed forces. The youngest was too young to fight, but when he saw that his two brothers were forced to fight, he fled to Australia, where he lived happily for several years.

What Jean did remember was the small one bedroom apartment the five of them shared with their parents, so poor and poverty stricken, suffering the outcome before, during, and then after the war, forced to use food stamps and fighting simply just to survive with what they had, which wasn't much. They lived in a very small town north of Toronto, which consisted mostly of farmland and few in population.

Before the outbreak of war, Jean was responsible

for looking after his brothers and sisters while his father searched desperately for work in a town he barely knew with very little luck. Times were tough, jobs were scarce, and their simple lives were an ominous challenge just to survive.

The war continuously took the lives of thousands of men who were forced to fight for their country, with the growing fear that Jean and his brothers wouldn't survive the physical or emotional consequences, should they be among the fortunate few to return home safely.

Black slavery was very well known at the time, so any rescues were kept very secretive within the town. Almost everyone was terrified to help those poor slaves searching for a better life. They had come up from the south and crossed at the Quebec border. Their owners were vicious, torturous, and worked them to near death in the cotton fields, threatening to kill their wives and children if they did not achieve what was expected of them each day. They lived in horror with many dropping dead from severe exhaustion and dehydration while their bodies were just tossed to the side like garbage. If caught, those who rescued them would also be prosecuted to the fullest extent of the law, or worse.

There was one exception with the courageous efforts of a woman in the town who would help them escape. She was unafraid of the consequences, and so dedicated to protecting them with the mercy that others were to afraid to give.

Rosie would be the one heroine in her town with the unspoken words of what she did for them, but everyone knew and praised her for her courage and dedication, committed to protecting her in every way they could. They all admired her without having the bravery to do it themselves. It would be many years before the truth finally came out and the amazing story would be told. I felt honored to have heard it straight from her mouth when I ran away from home at a very young age, and actually saw for myself what she had done; the sacrifices she made, the great lengths she went to, and the significant difference she made in those people's lives. She was fearless and it was mind-blowing as I listened intently to her tell the story.

The tunnel she had built under her house extended for five hundred yards from the back fields leading to a secret entrance into her basement. The false-paneled walls built inside her home hid the entrance to where she had housed them on the second floor. You almost had to walk sideways to climb the very narrow staircase where they slept and stayed most of the day, for fear the authorities would make an unannounced visit.

The antique piano in her living room was obviously broken if you tried to play it. It had been modified so that when four selected keys were played in rapid succession, it would release one of the false walls that would open up, leading to that narrow staircase. Upstairs, there were four bedrooms each supplying bunk beds that could house twenty adults and cots for their children if needed. The town's people were amazed at what she had done and how she had done it. The preparation in renovating her home had to be not only perfectly accurate, but it also had to mimic a normal residence from both the inside and outside, to evade suspicion.

No one had ever saved Jean from the poverty and pain his family had suffered, so he silently hoped that these escapees would be caught. This was probably why his intense prejudice carried on throughout his entire life and tried to inflict the same on his family and whoever else would listen to him. Jean was just prejudiced to the core. Everyone knew it, and therefore refused to talk about it when he was present.

As his family grew, so did his responsibility to help raise his siblings. He was at his uttermost limit with the fear of going to war and the repulsive reputation he had made for himself in town. It was everyone's opinion that he would inevitably plummet over the emotional edge at some point, and they all agreed that it would be sooner rather than later.

Many days, Jean would leave their apartment just to protect the little sanity he knew he had left. He would walk drudgingly for hours through the northern snow, just trying to understand his thoughts about where he was going in life, what he really wanted, and if he could ever be free from the insidious comments made about him behind his back. He worried wondering if he would ever find anything to make him happy.

Jean knew that the war would be damaging to him both emotionally and physically with the horrific deaths he would see and the work he would be forced to do for his country. He would lose many of the friends he met while fighting, and it would be very hard for him to overcome the repulsion of war. He tried to hide his fears from his family whenever possible, or as much as he thought he could, but his family knew he was different than most children growing up and feared the worst, when and if he ever returned home.

He would talk about the war in depth to us children for years. As small children, hearing such devastating horrors about the killings, bombings, and those who barely survived without their limbs, and permanent emotional damage, scarred us beyond reason. It wasn't that we just couldn't listen to it anymore, it was as if the war was all that he could hold on to in his life, and everyone had a moral obligation to bow down to him for his service to our country.

During a snowstorm on his walk one day toward

the pond everyone skated on, his attention was drawn to this beautiful woman he had seen several times before, but that day, he made a point of trying to meet her. She was as spectacular in character as she was to watch. She was in the middle of the pond twirling around with her obvious skating skills when he attempted to walk atop of the pond toward her. When he fell, his heart pounded as he saw her skating over to help him up. As she reached out and took his hand, she lost her balance and fell beside him smiling that beautiful smile he had seen so many times watching her with her friends. They both laughed as he thanked her. He was mesmerized by her gorgeous green eyes, which radiated with life when she smiled. She was a beautiful, petite young woman, and he was an attractive young man. They were nearly the same age, he soon found out as they sat there and talked while others skated around them as if they weren't there. There was magic in both their eyes as he climbed to a kneeling position and took her hand, trying to stand. Jean was unsteady on his feet, and as he tried to help pull her up, he fell again with her beautifully sculpted body landing on top of him. They smiled at each other and laughed once again. His eyes were locked on her face, and with the two of them looking deeply into each other's eyes, he knew that she felt what he was feeling.

This time, the young woman, Edith, rose to her

feet and used her blades to steady her as she helped him up. They both headed to the bench, continuing to laugh at what had just happened. As they sat on the bench, he told her that he had noticed her many times skating but didn't have the nerve to speak to her until then. Edith blushed, wondering silently to herself how she had never met this adorable, sweet man before that day.

They spoke for hours at the pond before he asked to meet her later that evening to continue their conversation, explaining that he was shipping off in the morning to go to war. Edith became infatuated with this man, whom she felt she could possibly love, and spend the rest of her life with. She thought of the beautiful children they could have in a fairytale life together. It was love at first sight. The fact that she barely knew him had never entered her thoughts, but it was a mistake she would soon regret.

Edith lived in the backwoods with her mother, Margaret, who was not well, and her father, Phillip, who was a hunter, surviving on the food he caught and selling the animal pelts for money to support his family. Edith was an amazing daughter and had a good job with the government that she loved. When she wasn't working, she was taking care of her mother while her father hunted. The little money she did make barely covered the cost of her mother's medications and the salve for her legs, which were badly afflicted with sores that were constantly infected. Over time, her legs became grossly disfigured, making it hard for her to walk. She was so ill that she spent long periods of time in the nearest hospital with Edith unable to visit due to the distance she would have to travel to get there and her job, which she needed to pay for the medical costs.

Jean and Edith got along so well, but then again, everyone in town loved Edith. On the other hand, Jean was severely disliked by the entire town, but they never voiced their opinions of him to Edith. They knew she was in love with him and to compromise their relationship would only hurt her. They stayed silent with the belief that Edith would soon realize the truth about him, and they would be there for her when the relationship collapsed.

As a sociopath, Jean knew what he was doing; he knew how to pick his victims and how to win them over. He knew that becoming the kind of person she could love, he would soon have full control over her without her suspecting anything that he didn't want her to know about him.

It would take awhile before Edith finally realized what she had done after marrying him, with his violent temper, contempt, and evil characteristics not only toward her but also their future children. Edith's first-born son died from one of Jean's attacks, and their next born, Leanne, would inherit her father's demonic traits, as time would soon tell. Her next and last child, Stephanie, was sweet and free from both their malicious characteristics. She was worth saving, but without the help she needed, Stephanie would soon discover that she was the only help she had for herself, and she had a vicious fight ahead of her if she was to survive.

The next morning, Jean was shipped off to war with Edith fearing that she would never see him again. She wrote him every day but never knew if he had received her letters. She faithfully promised to wait for him until his four-year tour was finished and they could start their fairytale life together. Hearing those words made Jean the happiest he had ever been.

Edith waited sometimes weeks before getting a response from Jean. She would sit perched outside the post office daily before work, waiting anxiously for a letter from him. When she did get a letter, he spoke of all the rat-infested foxholes he was forced to live in, the radar stations he was responsible for building, the dysentery that too many suffered under such extreme conditions, and the lack of food available. It frightened her to near death worrying about him, but she would always be positive about his safe return.

When he was finishing his tour, Jean wrote to say he would be returning to her soon and proposed right there in his letter. Edith was ecstatic and waited at the train station for him to arrive every day, taking time off from work and hoping she would be the first person he saw when exiting the train. She had made herself a new dress when she received his last letter, hoping that it would make him happy to see how it outlined her perfect figure. It was a light-green color that accentuated her gorgeous eyes and perfectly contoured frame that he loved so much.

When the train finally pulled into the station two weeks later, Jean was one of the fifteen soldiers who returned. Many were on crutches, and some had lost their limbs, while their comrades pushed them off the train in wheelchairs. Edith waited anxiously to see if Jean had come back in one piece or if he would return without his legs or arms. She wondered how she would react, bracing herself for the worst. She was so relieved when she saw Jean jump off the train in his uniform with every part of his body still intact. She felt so bad for those who came back in pieces, knowing most of them who lived there in town. It was a day to remember, and she had never been happier to see the man she loved return in one piece.

It wasn't long after his return that they were married right there in town by the mayor, who was also the justice of the peace and a dear friend. The entire town had attended but mostly because of Edith and not Jean. Edith was gorgeous in the white wedding dress that she had made herself. Her father was there to give her away, but her mother had recently been taken to the hospital, this time with life-threatening pneumonia, and was unable to attend.

After the war, Jean had become more distant with those around him in town. He had an attitude that made many shy away from him whenever possible. They assumed that it was from the war, but because of his behavior prior to the war, no one was really sure. He was just very sketchy, self-absorbed, and not a conversationalist by any means. It seemed as though he was hiding something of himself from everyone, yet Edith couldn't see it and never understood what her friends were trying to tell her, so she made up excuses for him, and he avoided any kind of contact with them.

After they were married, Jean went back to school and got his degree. They lived with her parents in their one-room house outside of town, isolated deep within the woods. It was far enough away from the town and its people, who hated him, but they always feared for their wonderful friend, who wasn't thinking clearly about her husband and the peril he was capable of creating.

Once Jean graduated, he told Edith that the only way they could grow together as a couple was to move to the city of Toronto, where the job opportunities were endless and the money was so much better. There, they could buy their first home and start a family together. In reality, Jean had to get his wife away from the poison that the townspeople would eventually fill her mind with, and this was the perfect reasoning he could hide behind.

With Edith able to transfer to her same job position in Toronto, Jean landed a job at a prestigious accounting firm. They found a house in east Toronto that they could afford with both salaries combined. The house was perfect for them in a nice quiet neighborhood close to both their jobs. It would be a new start for them both, in a place where no one would know anything about them, and Jean could feel safe with the freedom he needed to get what he wanted in life.

Shortly after the move, Edith became friends with everyone almost immediately, against Jean's orders for them to keep to themselves. She joined the local church and was very popular with everyone there, both in her neighborhood and the church. Jean, in contrast, kept to himself for fear of being exposed for who he really was. Jean loved his wife and his new job, and he knew together they would be very happy if she would just do what she was told.

They both lived happily for awhile before Edith announced that she was pregnant. Jean tried to look excited at the news, but secretly, it was not something that he was thrilled about. It meant that he would have to share his wife with not only the neighbors and the church, but now with a child who would take up the remainder of their time together. His mind raced with the thoughts of the pregnancy; the whining, extra cost, crying throughout the night, and breast feeding. Now, this new baby would interrupt the plans he had since he was a child after his mother was mysteriously murdered, and her killer never found. He smiled at the thought, remembering how the bitch had forced him to raise his siblings when he should have been playing and having fun with the other kids his own age. He was proud of that accomplishment, and knew that no one would ever discover the truth surrounding her death.

Edith was very happy. As the pregnancy continued, and her stomach grew bigger, she was making the most beautiful baby and maternity clothes, which she loved to do. Jean, on the other hand didn't approve of all her time being spent doing the many things that did not include him, so his temper started to show more and more often. Edith noticed the change, but Jean convinced her that it was her hormones taking over, that he had not changed one bit, and that after the baby was born, they would go back to being normal, and their life would be great. It didn't take much to convince her that he was right, and she was being ridiculous with such nonsense.

It was four months into the pregnancy when she got word that her father had been killed while hunting in the woods back home. It was an unfortunate accident with her father forgetting to wear his bright hunting jacket that told other hunters he was in the area. Edith was horrified at the news and quickly called Jean at work to tell him what had happened, and that she was on her way to the train station to go home.

Jean was angry that she would actually go without him before getting his permission for the trip first. He wouldn't be there to protect her from those vultures in the town who would possibly keep her from returning to him. He was becoming frantic, but in a sympathetic tone, he told her that he was leaving the office right then, he would pick her up at home, and they would go together. Edith just thought that he was being thoughtful, supportive, and considerate of her, especially in her condition. The cab that she had called was already en route to the house so they agreed to meet at the train station.

Jean's boss was very sympathetic, when he claimed that it would be too much for his pregnant wife to do on her own in her condition. He gladly gave Jean the time off under the circumstances as Jean raced out of the office in fear of missing her at the train station.

Edith barely had enough time to pack a few of Jean's things before the cab arrived, but she did get to the station in time to find Jean waiting for her. He was irritated because she had never discussed the trip with him before leaving, and it showed. Edith was in tears at his attitude, and the first time she had seen that kind of controlling insensitivity in him. Her father had just died for heaven's sake, and her poor mother was left there alone without any help. Edith knew she couldn't make the funeral arrangements on her own, or even afford the high cost involved. She needed to be there for her, and no one was going to take that away from her.

As they arrived at the station, nearly the entire town was there to meet her, stunned to see that Jean had also come with her. Her best friend would put them up in their beautiful home, dead center in the middle of town. The two had been best friends since kindergarten, and her friend wouldn't hear of her going to any motel in town, especially in her condition. Edith was still worried, and disparaged as she departed from the train. The first words her friend conveyed was that her mother was being looked after by a family friend who was staying with her while she recovered. Edith was so grateful for the information, and that she had friends she could count on when she couldn't be there.

Edith and Jean unpacked their things in one of the most gorgeous rooms they had ever seen. As soon as they finished, Edith wanted to go to see her mother, but without Jean. With such a family tragedy, she knew it would be best if it was just her; bringing the man her mother despised would just make matters worse. Of course, she never told Jean what her mother thought of him and needed to approach him in a different way so it would be his idea for her to go there without him.

When she arrived at the house, the family friend led Edith into the living room, telling her that her mom was very sick and that she wouldn't be able to stay too long. Her own husband had taken ill and she needed to be there for him, so this would be the last day she could stay. Edith slid down onto the nearest chair with her head buried in her hands, wondering what she could do to resolve the situation before her. The only solution was to have her mother move in with her and Jean at their Toronto home. The hospital would be close by, and there were ambulances that would come faster when needed. There were so many better specialists there who could help her mother, and as she stood up, she made up her mind that this was the way it would be, whether Jean liked it or not. How she would break the news to Jean was another story, and would require a lot of time and thought with how she would approach him.

After supper that night, as Edith was still sitting at the dinner table, Jean excused himself to go outside on the front porch for a smoke while she continued to get caught up with everyone at the table. They too were grief-stricken at the circumstances but told her that the entire town had contributed to the cost of her father's funeral. The funeral director himself was there for dinner and had discounted the cost of the funeral so that it could be covered by the amount her friend had collected.

Long before Edith married and moved to Toronto, she had been making monthly payments for her family's three graves, a total cost of $600 over a three year period. It had taken her the entire three years to pay them off, but at the time, it was just the three of them that mattered, and she felt comfortable knowing that they would all be buried together. She never anticipated that she would fall in love, get married, and leave the town she loved and grew up in.

Edith was very appreciative at what her friends had done for her with the funeral costs. She was so excited that she left the table to go out to the porch to tell Jean right away. She couldn't get the words out fast enough before Jean threw his cigarette halfway across the yard, standing up in another fury that she had never seen before. He barked at her that they were not a charity case, and he wouldn't have any of that in his life. He was irate, on fire, and had gone way too far this time. He reached out and pushed Edith, not realizing his own strength, as if a reaction one might have being caught off guard during the war. Edith flew down the stone porch stairs. She was bent over in agonizing pain, causing enough noise that everyone from the dining table rushed out to see what the terrible screaming and thumping was about.

Totally humiliated, Edith stood up and told her friends that she had lost her balance and fallen down the stairs. Jean had apologized before they came, trying to help her to her feet. Edith was dumbfounded, saying she was okay, and that she was just embarrassed and wanted to go to bed. Jean looked at them very calmly and seemingly sympathetic, suggesting he help her to their room.

Once in the room, Jean apologized again, saying that he didn't know what had come over him, and that he was terribly sorry for what he had done. He continued to say that her friends collecting for the funeral were extremely thoughtful with what they were doing for her. Jean still had to come up with a reasonable explanation for the attack. He quickly thought for a moment before trying adamantly to convince her that he had had an appalling flashback from the war, and that it could be the only reason he would ever do such an unbearable thing to the woman of his dreams.

Edith took him in her arms and held him while he pretended to sob uncontrollably, not noticing that there were no tears flowing from his eyes, but believing the war excuse he gave just the same. Only a monster would do that to her, and she could never think that the man she truly loved would ever do such a horrific thing to her on purpose.

Jean helped her change into her night-gown, noticing the trickle of blood between her legs but saying nothing to her about it. Silently, he thought that this could be the answer to his problem of sharing her with that child embedded in her belly that he never wanted. They both lay on the bed as he doted on her, hoping to recover from what he had done while convincing her that it was only an accident he would always regret.

They both fell asleep until Jean woke up in the middle of the night with Edith screaming in pain and the bed sheets saturated with an overabundance of blood now flowing between her legs. Within minutes, the room was swarming with their friends, reacting to her screams from their bedrooms at the opposite side of the house.

Her friend's son, Harry, immediately ran out to the barn and bridled one of the horses, taking off as fast as he could for Doc Caldwell's home across town. By the time Doc returned with Harry, Edith was in horrific pain and still bleeding profusely, lying there almost lifeless from the loss of so much blood. Jean was frantic at the amount of blood everywhere. It flowed like a river until Jean thought that he might lose his wife when all he wanted was to lose the baby. This was not part of his plan, and it was all he could think about as everyone was ushered out of the room for Doc to try to save her life.

After what seemed like hours, Doc emerged from the bedroom, slowly shaking his head and telling everyone that it was a question of time to see if she would survive. Edith had lost so much blood as well as their little baby boy. Jean was contemptuous at the news, accusing Doc of not doing his job properly while vigorously trying to hide what he had done when Doc asked what had happened.

Jean never once considered that his baby might be a boy. That would have been the most wonderful child for him, someone he could groom from birth, teaching him the true reality about the world, and who would someday carry on the King name.

Doc had given Edith a sedative after the news that her baby boy was dead. It was the last scream everyone heard as Doc left the bedroom to console Jean, and confirmed the news with those who patiently waited to hear.

Doc stayed the night, overseeing Edith's care, and called the hospital to say that his patient would be there first thing in the morning. Unfortunately, there weren't any ambulances close by so it was up to the rescue choppers to fly in and transport the seriously injured to the nearest hospital ninety miles east of town. It was a tough night for county rescues with only one chopper covering several miles, and their arrival in the morning was the only option.

Early the next morning, the chopper finally landed in the wheat fields behind the house. Edith was still terribly weak and needed a blood transfusion as soon as possible. She was carried onto a stretcher and into the chopper with her best friend at her side. Jean refused to ride in the helicopter, claiming flashbacks from the war, and insisted on taking the train to the hospital. He wasn't taking any chances and packed all of their things so he could take his wife directly from the hospital back home to Toronto, with the promise that he would take very good care of her.

No one was happy with that decision, but then they didn't want him staying there himself longer than he had to and offered to drive him to the station. To say that they hated Jean was an understatement. His explanation of what happened on the porch didn't make sense to any of them. Edith had spent seventeen years treading up and down those same stairs in the worst kinds of weather with no problems. They continuously looked at Jean suspiciously until the train pulled out that morning, knowing that there had to be something else that contributed to her fall. They were convinced that it was Jean; the same way the authorities thought that Jean was responsible for his mother's death but had no solid evidence to arrest him.

The hospital kept Edith for a week, monitoring her for any further problems. Some of the bruising could have easily been attributed to the fall, but there was other bruising that seemed suspicious to the doctors. If it weren't for Jean spending the entire week at her side, and sleeping in the chair next to her in the room, it might have sparked a concern. Jean was good at what he did, and knew that this experience would somehow work to his advantage in the future. He was proud of his deceptive skills and felt invincible. He played the perfect husband and was happy when it was time to take Edith home.

It was a very long train ride back to Toronto, and another twenty-minute cab ride to their house, so they were both exhausted when they arrived. Jean had to work the next day, so they went to bed early after Jean made his wife a light dinner with whatever was left in the fridge, and then helped her to the bedroom.

They woke up in the morning after a restful sleep, and Edith was adamant about Jean going back to work. She insisted she would be fine and her good friend down the street would come and spend the day with her until he got home. That terrified Jean, thinking that she might say something to her friend about what actually did happen to her and their baby.

Jean was exhibiting obvious signs of an abuser; keeping his victim secluded from friends and family and always keeping her by his side when they were out in public. What Jean didn't know was that Edith had made arrangements for her mother to soon follow them to Toronto once she was feeling better and able to travel. It was not an easy subject to bring up with Jean's recent behavior, so she kept it to herself until the time was right to tell him.

Jean's first day back to work was long and stressful as he worried about what was happening back at his house. He called every half hour with her friend answering each time. She refused to let Jean talk to his wife, telling him that she was resting and she didn't want to wake her. Finally, he left work early and made his way home on the bus. Times were tough, so the added expense of a car wasn't in his plan yet. Once off the bus, he hurried home, and as he entered the house, Edith's friend stopped him dead in his tracks, saying that the doctor had just been in to see Edith and had given her a sedative. Jean was furious that he wasn't called about the doctor coming. He ordered her friend to get out of his house and to never come back again. He would care for his wife without her or for that matter anyone else in the neighborhood who felt the need to destroy their lives.

Jean's boss wasn't as understanding or sympathetic when he was asked for more time off after the trip. It wasn't only the additional time he asked for, but more so his attitude toward everyone in the office. Jean had been unnecessarily offensive to everyone on a daily basis, so he was given an ultimatum that if he took more time he would have to find another job.

Jean threw the phone across the room after yelling at his boss to go to hell. The commotion woke Edith up, and as she entered the dining room, she couldn't help but notice the phone pulled out of the wall and the mirror smashed as the phone made contact with it. For the second time, Edith was becoming more frightened with what was happening to her husband. Jean calmed down long enough to notice her, and as he walked toward her, he told her that his boss wasn't happy with him because of the time he took off for her father's death. Edith felt terrible that she had caused such a catastrophic situation and held her husband close; apologizing once again for the trouble she had caused their family. Jean accepted the hug, and when he knew she couldn't see his face, he smiled slightly again at his accomplishment to make her feel guilty.

Edith promised that she would get better and return to work by the end of the week regardless of the doctor telling her to stay in bed for two more weeks. Jean, of course, was happy with her returning to work without him having to tell her the truth about losing his job. He was semi-confident that he would find another job, but with his wife working full-time and making a good salary, he felt that she at least owed him that much after all the sacrifices he had made for her. With a frown, he then realized he wouldn't be able to give his last boss as a reference because of his arrogance, obnoxious behavior, and the inability to work well with others. Then, it was as if a light went off in his head. Reaching for his briefcase, he rifled through to find a blank company letterhead to write his own recommendation. Jean smiled at the thought for being smarter than he was given credit for.

Edith returned to work as promised against doctor's advice. Jean would get up every morning, saying that he was going to the job he didn't have, and was always home every afternoon when Edith arrived. She never noticed the change in his hours when he usually got home later than she did. She was just thankful that her husband had forgiven her for what she thought was all her fault.

Life continued on more peacefully since Jean had stopped working, but while still unemployed, he mentioned that they needed to buy a car if they were going to continue evolving in their life, and the car was necessary for his work. Edith agreed, and in less than an hour, a new car was delivered and parked outside in their driveway with the sticker still on the windshield.

Edith always had a positive attitude about what Jean did for them, convinced that he did everything for her, so she never questioned his decisions, or asked for an explanation. He was very generous with forgiving her for all the problems he made her believe she had caused, and used them often when he felt he was losing control over her. She refused to see Jean for what he truly was, so she continued being the perfect little wife she knew he always wanted, and thought she could help his outbursts change, if only she was good enough.

After the confrontation at the house with her friend, the neighbors kept their distance, fearing not only for Edith but also for themselves. Each time she was at church, she could almost hear the whispers being said behind her back. She chalked it up to gossip and refused to accept what everyone was accusing her husband of being; a psychopathic monster. She became very lonely and isolated, but her job as a wife was to make her husband happy, and to be totally committed to him. The harder she tried, the better Jean became, and their life together seemed to be improving, until it wasn't.

When Edith announced that she was pregnant again, Jean was thrilled at the thought of having another boy. The pregnancy was a good experience for them both with no problems until the doctor told them that they were having a baby girl. Jean had flown into another rage after finding out it wasn't going to be the boy he desperately wanted. Of course, he blamed Edith for the injustice. He claimed she did it on purpose just to spite him, but she was so happy that her baby would be healthy, beautiful, and the most adorable baby in the nursery.

Her name was Leanne, and she was as beautiful as predicted. Unfortunately, Leanne would inherit her father's malicious and sadistic characteristics, thus becoming the catalyst who would change their lives forever; more specifically, her soon-to-be-born sister, Stephanie.

CHAPTER 2

It was a cold and blistery February day in 1959, with the wind blowing through the streets of Toronto at maximum speed. The snow-banks were layered on the ground, whispering uncertain danger to any who attempted to cross through them, with a treacherous undercoating of black ice below.

Cars weaved through the streets while the snow pounded heavily onto windshields, making it difficult to see through the huge flakes that covered the car's glass as the wipers fought furiously to clear them with each swipe of the blade. School buses and public transportation were cancelled, and vehicles had come to a complete standstill while the streets were bombarded with the mounds of snow that gave Canadian winters their nefarious reputation. It was not a day to be reckoned with, but people's lives moved on just the same.

A little girl's mother lay in labor, whimpering atop the soaked wet bed sheets. The moans quickly turned into screeching cries that emanated throughout the entire house. Her mother woke from the pains of each contraction with her unborn child, signifying the time had now come for this baby girl to leave the comfort and safety of her womb. Now the task was getting her to the hospital on time and fighting the horrific conditions awaiting them outside their suburban home.

The intensity of the contractions had only just started to increase, and she was unable to bridle the moans that had also wakened her husband, who was now sitting up in bed agitated by the disturbance from such a restful sleep. Unsure as to what was happening, he growled, turning away from her, and threw back the covers, disappearing into the bathroom like he had on the many other mornings during the last trimester of her pregnancy. It was several hours earlier than usual, and in no uncertain terms, he had made it clear that he was disturbed by the rude awakening. As the bathroom door closed behind him, he could hear her apologizing emphatically once again for this mistake she knew could easily ruin everyone's day, even under the circumstances of bringing his baby girl into the world. She fought back tears at the disturbing thought she knew too well.

Just then, their bedroom door flew open, and her five-year-old daughter galloped fearlessly across the room and jumped onto the bed at high speed, singing the "Snowy Day" song. It was a ritual her daughter loved dearly after each fresh snowfall. It meant that she got to play outside, make snow angels, and build funny snowmen with her mother all day long without a care in the world after her father left for work.

It wasn't long before the reality set in, the song ended abruptly, and the smile faded from her face as she searched the room for her father, asking if he too would be having a snow day from work. With Daddy home, it always meant that she had to play quietly in her room alone, so he would be undisturbed by the fun she loved when he wasn't around. There would be no funny snowmen and no snow angels on those days, and she became withdrawn as her brow tightened at the mere thought beginning to show across her saddening face.

Almost as if she anticipated her daughter's reaction, Edith smiled as she sat her daughter next to her on the bed. "Today is a very special day, Leanne," she started to explain, as she took her daughter's hands and placed them softly over her huge belly as the baby kicked with all her might.

Leanne jumped back with a confused expression on her face. She had never felt the baby kick so hard in the past few months and wondered what was happening. Edith continued to tell her that it was time that her baby sister came out into the world to meet her, and this was the day it would happen.

Leanne sat back, trying to understand the only way a five-year-old could imagine with how a baby would do this. Would it come out of her mommy's mouth? Leanne wondered, gagging at the thought. With each new thought came a new expression on her face, which quickly changed, and then her face grew dark and withdrawn as she looked down at the soaked bed sheets beneath her on the bed. "You pee-peed the bed, Mommy, but that's okay; I've done that too," Leanne whispered to her in an embarrassed tone.

Edith smiled at her daughter's innocence and the compassion she showed as she spoke. Just then, as the bathroom door swung open, they both jumped back as if being caught doing something neither one was allowed to do. Edith quickly ordered Leanne back to her bedroom the way she had done so many times before, telling her that they would finish their talk later. Leanne knew too well what that meant and bolted off out of sight for fear of his usual punishment for her invading their bedroom without his invitation.

As the bedroom door closed behind her, she could hear her mother quickly deny any wrong-doing by her daughter in a tone that was not comforting to hear. The conversation was interrupted by the pain of another contraction, and as Leanne sneaked quickly back to her room, she could hear the groans from that contraction, and they frightened her. As Leanne lay back on her bed, she kept reminding herself with what her father had told her about this new baby sister, and how he said that this baby would affect her life now in so many different ways. Her thoughts were now festering into hate, without realizing what it really meant.

When her little friend down the street got her baby brother, there was nothing but total chaos, with yelling and crying each time she was there. Leanne was always happy to say good-bye and go home. Her friend's baby brother got *all* the attention while her friend was so easily discarded and pushed to the side. On a good day at best, in her own home with her parents, Leanne recalled the fear from all the fighting, yelling, and crying as she buried her head under the covers at the thought of more to come. All she could think of was that the love she did receive would soon disappear completely, to make room for the creepy thing who would now become a new part of their family, and take the rest of what she did have, away from her. She already hated the thought, regardless of the many pep talks her mother gave her over the course of her tummy swelling.

"This will be a life-changing situation," her father kept repeating to her at every opportunity. It was one that she would have to fight to the death, just to keep her from being discarded like she saw happening to her friend.

The weekday morning ritual of patiently waiting for the front door to open and close for her father to leave for work seemed endlessly longer this day. Leanne loved the mornings when her mother, shortly after the front door closing, would peer into her room with the door slightly ajar, making funny faces that started the day off with a smile. Edith would come into her bedroom to play, and then they would make breakfast together, which she loved so much, but this day was different. There were no smiles, no funny faces, no playing, or even anything to eat for breakfast. The silence in the house was bewitching except for the intermittent groans of pain that seemed to get louder as she hid and listened from under her bed sheets.

This was the day that Leanne had feared the most, and now it had finally come. It would be a day that no one would come to her side or include her in anything that was happening. No front door would open and close when her father went to work, and she felt scared at what would become of her. She just sat alone in silence, listening and hoping for that door to close, but it never did. It was to be the day she would always remember, the day when her sister was born and ruined everything that she loved in her life.

By noon, Leanne was so hungry from not having breakfast but still too scared to leave her room. Suddenly, her bedroom door swung open with her father shouting and grabbing at her in a panic to move quickly. It was time to go to the hospital. Leanne tried to protest his plan in the way most five-year-olds would do by retaliating and then trying to hide from him, mostly because of the knotted pain in her stomach, but it wasn't up for an argument she would win. He pulled her quickly from her room to her waiting mother, whose face was now contorted into expressions she had never seen before. Leanne was horrified, but there was no time for that now as her father rushed them both to the front door.

The weather was now in full blizzard mode with the snow that had fallen throughout the night, making it difficult to dig their way out of the driveway, and get to the hospital on time. All the ambulances were out on emergency calls, stating a minimum fifty-minute wait. Regardless, Jean continued bellowing into the phone to the operator, as the rage inside him increased, demanding immediate help. It was their second living child, and the contractions were now only two minutes apart. It was no secret she had lost the first child, and with Leanne who was breach with complications beyond Edith's control, it was something they did not want repeated with this child without medical assistance. Edith's doctor gave explicit instructions for her to keep the anxiety to a minimum, but as her husband's panic accelerated, so did his inability to control the situation, and he was becoming enraged, almost demonic. The beast they both knew and feared could easily be released under these strenuous conditions.

Edith sat silently between contractions, glaring into the comforting space as she had taught herself to do, recalling the happy news the day her doctor told her she was pregnant at age forty. During this new pregnancy, Edith's husband had changed for the better, and Edith thrived in this wonderful new relationship with him. The arguments had significantly subsided, and he had become the semi-docile man she had first met, fallen in love with, and married. Reluctantly, her mind traveled to the reason why as she tried to accept it as just a new positive chapter in their lives. What if he changed back again and exhibited the demonic and destructive characteristics she feared after she brought this new baby girl into the world, like he had done with Leanne? He had blamed her for the first miscarriage with the son they could have had, and constantly reminded her of it. It was her only thought as fear crossed her face, trying to dismiss the uncertainty as another contraction began, replacing her thoughts with pain.

As they both waited in anticipation of an ambulance, the next-door neighbor suddenly appeared at their door after watching Edith's husband scramble nervously to clear the drifts of snow that had fallen onto their driveway overnight. Their street was untouched by the snow plows that continuously fought to clear the main streets first, and there was no time with this amount of snow, even in this dire crisis, for their secondary street to be cleared.

Their neighbor rushed fearlessly to the surrounding houses, pounding on doors for assistance, shouting that their dear friend and neighbor needed help. With Edith being so well liked by everyone on the street, her friends became the rescue team that would make getting to the hospital possible to achieve. Within minutes, another neighbor across the street appeared in his four-by-four truck, modified with oversized tires, still dressed in his pajamas, and was waiting at their door to rush Edith to the hospital in time.

The drive to the hospital was treacherous with the windshield wipers unable to remove the enormous flakes as they hit the glass. Extreme stress was not something Edith's husband handled well, although he was great at creating it on more occasions than she cared to recall.

Just how much were her neighbors aware of what her husband was really like? Edith had her suspicions but quickly pushed the thoughts from her mind. They were her neighbors, and she knew very well that gossip traveled very quickly on their street. She worked hard to keep her secret safe, hoping that she hid it well but always wondering if they could see through his deception and the many lies she told them, and herself. Would Jean also be the reason that this child died too, like her first son, whom he had killed with his behavior and physical attack on her back home? She could only pray that with so many people now involved, that she and her children would be safe.

The car swerved with each new contraction, in unison with the screams that pierced their ears in the cab of the truck. As the contractions grew closer, the agonizing screams got louder. Leanne watched as her mother withered in pain, hoping that they wouldn't get to the hospital in time for this vile creature to be born. This venomous thing that made her mother suffer so terribly would also destroy her life quickly. She sat quietly in the truck with her hands over her ears and her mind racing with ideas. She may have been five years old, but she had the sinister mind of an adult, capable of anything she put her mind to, which she obviously inherited from her father.

Finally, Edith's husband announced that the hospital was coming into sight, trying to reassure the woman he married that it would all be all right and that there was no need for the continued fear she persistently brought to his attention. He was glad he had called ahead before leaving the house, so the nurses and gurney would be waiting for them at the entrance as soon as they arrived. As they sped into the ER entrance, there was no gurney and no help in sight. Leanne's father grew angrier with every second at the hospital's negligence. The dead, dark look growing within his eyes was a very familiar one to Edith, the one that she had prayed and hoped had been gone for good. The fierce look on his face was totally visible and quickly progressing from the intense stress surrounding them. The fact that the hospital had disobeyed his explicit orders to be ready when they arrived was all that was needed to trigger the beast within him.

Anger was something that Leanne knew very well with her father's temper. She had seen it often enough to know that when his lips were pursed tightly together, his eyes were clouded over, and the orders bellowed from his mouth in that ferocious tone, there was no hope for whatever or whoever was obstructing his path, and it was best just not to be seen or heard.

Total havoc would ensue, but her mother would usually redirect the attention away from her daughter by safely sending her to her room, and receiving the full force of his fury onto herself. It was a ritual she could recall occurring often, and she was made to listen to it behind the confines of her closed bedroom door, hoping that it would soon pass.

Once the car came to a complete stop, her father ran to the flashing lights of the emergency room doors, shouting commands for quick action to their immediate needs. An orderly appeared with the gurney and her mother was quickly placed upon it, and whisked away at full speed in excruciating pain. Leanne sat in the freezing cold, responding to her dad's demands to stay put and wait for him to return. When he didn't return, she began to panic and cry, thinking back to her friend who was also forgotten.

Finally, after what seemed like forever to a child, Leanne exited the car and walked toward the huge doors as her father had done. An ambulance had just arrived, and hospital staff immediately emerged, surrounding their vehicle while pushing her aside in an attempt to save the life of the patient who lay motionless on the ambulance bed.

It was then that one of the nurses crouched down to Leanne, introducing herself in a calming voice, asking her name and why she was all alone. This nurse had no idea who she was or where she had come from, and Leanne cried uncontrollable sobs of fear, unable to speak to the nurse who was now holding her tightly in her arms. She picked up the little girl, clad only in her pajamas, and carried her into the building away from the horror and blinding cold.

Leanne was freezing, all alone in this huge white room the nurse led her to, swarmed by so many strangers around her. She was frightened by the patients covering their wounds, moaning and groaning, while hospital stuff bustled around them like buzzards circling dead carcasses, as she had seen once on TV. The nurse diverted Leanne's attention away from a man being brought in by his family bleeding from a kitchen knife accident, with his blood violently spurting out in every direction. The woman called to another nurse for assistance, but it was a busy night at the ER. They were short-staffed and on high alert with the traffic accidents caused by the fury of the storm. She placed Leanne in a chair, pleading with her to remain there until she returned. Leanne looked up at her with a somber nod and fearful eyes as a single tear ran down her cheek.

The hunger pains in Leanne's tummy were turning to nausea as she felt the vomit rise in her throat. She frantically searched the halls for a bathroom, but when she couldn't see one, she got up off her chair and scurried down the hall in search of it. She felt helpless as the many giants of all shapes and sizes passed her by. She managed to tug on some random woman's pant leg as she was passing by her, and looking up, she asked where she could find a bathroom. The woman pointed to a door at the far end of the hall by the elevator, directing her to the picture above the door. Leanne started to run toward the door but knew she wasn't going to make it in time. Just as she got to the pictured door, a wild rush of vomit spewed from her mouth like lava out of a volcano. She fell to the floor, holding her stomach with each wretch. From a distance, she could hear someone calling out to her, but it wasn't her mother's familiar voice she was hoping to hear. As she looked up from the floor, she could see the nurse who had put her in the chair hurrying towards her, relieved that she had found her. She was terribly concerned why this child was vomiting and had no idea she was as starved for food as she was for love and attention by her family.

They walked back down the hall together to the door her parents arrived at, only this time, the nurse stopped at the admitting desk to ask the receptionist if she had any idea of who the child was or whom she could be related to. The dark-haired woman peered up from the mound of paperwork, lowering her glasses, bewildered at the situation before her. When asked, Leanne had only mentioned that her mother was in terrible pain when her father brought her to the hospital. It never occurred to her that it would be so important to mention that her baby sister was about to be born. Then, when she was asked for her family name, Leanne replied as any five-year-old was expected to answer. "My name is Leanne, and my parents are Mommy and Daddy."

The women briefly gazed at each other questioningly as the child before them began to wretch again.

"I'm so hungry!" Leanne cried out. "Daddy

wouldn't let me eat breakfast this morning, and my tummy hurts."

The nurse was constantly searching the halls in expectation of someone looking for this lost little child, and when there was no one, she took her hand and told her softly that she would take her to a quiet room to clean the vomit from her face and clothes, and then she would take her to the cafeteria to get her some food. She solemnly asked Leanne if that would be okay, trying not to upset her more than she already was, standing before her so scared, innocent, and afraid of what was to become of her. It had been hours now since they arrived with time flying by among the hustle, bustle, and confusion of the ER department.

Leanne agreed happily and walked in silence with the nurse to an empty room, where she sat her on a bed and removed the excessive vomit that covered her. When she was finished, the nurse led Leanne back down the hall, passing the admitting desk, to the security office, where she asked if anyone had been looking for the girl. With the shake of the security guard's head indicating there were no inquiries, she briefly told him that she was taking the child to the cafeteria to get her food and would return shortly in case anyone asked about her.

Leanne sadly looked up to the nurse as she whimpered before speaking. "No one loves me anymore, and now my sister will be the only one they love."

The nurse peered down at her with saddened eyes, not quite understanding what the child was trying to say. Calmly, she proceeded to the cafeteria in hope that the truth would soon be revealed.

They arrived at the cafeteria, and Leanne couldn't believe how much food was laid out in a line of several platters that she could choose from. Her eyes lit up like those of a child in a candy store, and the nurse noticed it right away. As she pointed to each platter, the nurse smiled. She suggested the Jell-O tray to see if her stomach could tolerate it, and Leanne smiled as she nodded. Before they left, the nurse stopped by the counter for one more Jell-O to take with them and a promise that she would get her a sandwich from the meal tray when it was delivered shortly to the ER for patients. Leanne beamed at the thought of more food coming, loving the way this nurse spoke to her so calmly and gave her so much attention.

"I'll bring the Jell-O for my mommy," she said. "She's having a baby today, and her tummy is about to break open."

Bingo, the nurse thought as they exited the cafeteria. The missing parents now made more sense. They headed back toward the admitting department to find the room her mother had been assigned to.

As they walked down the hall, Leanne was content

and finally smiling happily from all the attention. It made her feel so wanted and loved until she heard that familiar gruff voice yelling from the end of the hall, shouting orders in that hostile tone that made her cringe at every spoken word. Without looking up, she murmured to the nurse that her father was there and pleaded with her not to leave her side.

Her father saw the two of them from a distance and shouted Leanne's name out again, the way he did when he was angry at her for something he thought she had done wrong. Leanne quickly hid behind the nurse the way she used to hide behind her mother when she was there to defend her. The nurse quickly noticed the change in her behavior as she gently clasped Leanne's hand tighter, squeezing three times as if to say it was going to be okay, but the nurse didn't know her father or what he was capable of.

The nurse stood still as the distance closed between them, with this man circling them like a vulture with his prey, angry that his daughter, who was instructed to stay where she was left, had defied his orders. The nurse had rescued her from the freezing cold with no coat on, but she noticed the look from her father and quickly stopped talking. It was reckless to leave a child in the freezing cold like he had done under such severe weather conditions, so she took a minute to compose herself before giving him a piece of her mind. This man gave off the worst vibes, and by his daughter's reaction, she knew it wasn't the first time he had done that.

Her father was very red in the face, with veins visibly showing in his forehead, maybe from anger or embarrassment, the nurse wasn't sure. She spoke calmly to him and told him that she had just returned from the cafeteria after getting his daughter some food for her empty tummy. She tightened her brow and forced a smile, refusing to give into his intimidation.

"That's beside the point!" her father growled in the same threatening tone that usually warded off anyone's attempt to question his control or authority.

He articulated each word like the roar of a bull with flailing arms, yelling at her as if it was her fault. "She was told to stay in the car until I returned, and she disobeyed me." He was furious that she would do such a thing. It wasn't an argument the nurse would win, and she knew it. No one could ever win when it came to facing this man's wrath if he felt it was deserved, and he had a way of showing that without question. It took all she had to stay calm, hoping it would soon pass with no collateral damage. In her twenty-two years of nursing, aside from her patients in the psych ward, this man had to be the poorest excuse of a human being she had ever encountered.

The security guard stood a short distance away, overhearing the conversation as the nurse gave an indication with her body language that his services might be needed should his hostility progress. He acknowledged with a quick nod and moved a little closer, pretending that he was not interested in them but just maneuvering throughout the halls as his job required him to do.

The nurse watched silently in contempt at her father's actions as he forcibly grabbed Leanne's hand and led her down the hall. The young child's head bowed as it usually did, as she tried vigorously to escape from the grasp that was obviously hurting her. As the nurse watched them veer around the corner, she thought about running after them, but just then, an orderly needing help caught her attention, and she turned to assist him with his lifeless patient, still thinking of that small, vulnerable child who begged her for help with pain-filled eyes, wondering what was happening in that little girl's life that scared her so terribly much.

As Leanne and her father reached the elevator heading to the obstetrics wing, Leanne turned to ask her dad if her mommy was going to be alright. In all the excitement, she had forgotten the reason for being there. Her father's mood changed, and his grasp lightened as he turned to her, attempting to be nice, telling her that she now had a baby sister. "This will be really nice for you, Leanne," he added. "You will have a sister to play with now; you will share your bedroom, toys, and games with her and you will take care of her throughout your entire life as a big sister". "She will be a loyal and trusting friend as you grow older together."

As they slowly got off the elevator and headed toward the delivery room, Leanne remembered her friend and how unhappy she was when her brother had been born. She wanted no part of it, but she would keep that a secret from everyone until she could figure out how to make her go away.

The shrieking cries from the many babies in the nursery they passed were piercing her ears as they walked down the hall to her mother's room. With her father's elevator speech still fresh in her mind, it sounded as if this was going to be the worst thing that could ever possibly happen to her. She sighed as they entered the room, and with a resentful look still in her eyes, she saw her new baby sister lying in her mother's arms, receiving the love that she should be having. Leanne perched herself up against the wall in the opposite corner across the room, feeling left out and unwanted.

Her thoughts were interrupted by her mother's smiling face. She was holding her sister, whom they named Stephanie, as she invitingly welcomed her daughter over to the bed. Leanne soon forgot the events of the day as her mother motioned for her again to come closer to meet her new sister. Leanne didn't want to say anything but thought silently that it was such an ugly thing, all wrinkled and red, and she hated her at first sight. Leanne's shoulders tensed in disgust at what she saw that made everyone so happy, except for her. Nonetheless, she obliged her mother's request, until she noticed a huge stuffed panda bear sitting lifelessly in the chair across the room, belonging to another mother.

Without hesitation, she ran to the chair to take a closer look, hoping no one would notice, with a look as if it was hers to take with her when she left. It was as if her father anticipated her actions and lashed out orders for her to "Stop!" Leanne instantly reacted and froze where she stood. She turned to see her mother's expression quickly change as she heard her softly repeat the invitation to come closer. The panda bear faded from her thoughts as she turned to face her mother as she spoke.

"Would you like to hold your new sister, sweetie?" her mother asked in an attempt to quickly change the mood that was becoming too intense around her. She felt it was important for her daughter to bond with Stephanie as soon as possible, for her to feel safe, and to be included in her sister's life.

Her father became overly concerned at such a stupid suggestion, and Leanne noticed the change in his body language immediately.

"No, Mummy, I'll just watch you," she replied as she edged closer toward the bed. "Are you okay now?"

Without thinking of her father's reaction, Leanne began to go into her childish ranting of the events that had happened to her earlier at the ER in the only way she knew how to express it. "I want to go home now, and I'm hungry, and a real nice nurse took care of me, and I was scared and threw up all over, and she cleaned me up and took me to a huge kitchen, and I was scared because you were gone and, and, and…" The dialogue was quickly interrupted by her father as it usually was when her childish gibberish and drama were more than he could take.

It was time to feed the baby, so they had to leave the room while the nurse helped her mother breast-feed for the first time. Leanne couldn't possibly understand the importance of this, so instead of any explanation as to why, she was happy to leave as fast as she could to get away from that disgusting thing they were giving so much attention to.

Childbirth was so different back in the day when it was not protocol for the father to be involved, and they were left to pace back and forth in the waiting room, waiting for the childbirth process to be finished. Breast-feeding was a matter between the mother and her baby. It required complete privacy, away from any distractions, and that meant husbands and siblings had to wait outside the room.

Leanne's father extended his hand out to Leanne, but she just ignored the suggestion, remembering how sore her hand had become while walking to the room with him. She passed by him, walking toward the door, her hands crossed against her chest and far enough away from him not to reach her. Once out in the hall, her father asked what she thought of her new baby sister. All Leanne could do was shrug at the thought as they continued to the waiting room. She turned toward her father and reluctantly nodded approval as they walked down the hall and into the elevator.

"Can we go to the huge kitchen here and eat, Daddy?" "My tummy feels sick and hungry," she asked as she unclasped her arms from her chest and rubbed her tummy.

"Okay, Leanne," her father replied. "Let's go and get an ice cream cone to celebrate. It will be our little secret."

That was great news to Leanne. Ice cream was one of her favorite foods, and she was rarely allowed to have it. The "secret" part wasn't anything she understood, what he meant when he said it, or, what he was suggesting. It would later unfold to be purely sick and perverse, but her sister, Stephanie, would be the one to tell the story. It would lead her into an entirely different world that she did not want, need, deserve, and there was nothing she could do about it. She would have to suffer; at least until she found the strength to fight, and win.

It had been a long day, and it was late into the night when Leanne and her dad arrived home, past Leanne's bedtime. She had been so tired that she had fallen asleep in the car. Being lost, forgotten, and scared had been exhausting, but she smiled slightly, remembering that wonderful nurse who took care of her and made her feel like the special princess she always knew that she was.

The smile was interrupted with her father's orders to wake up, get into the house, and go to bed! "But Mommy helps me brush my teeth and tells me a bedtime story before bed," she protested as her father just looked at her with disgust at the idea of fulfilling such a ridiculous, childish ritual.

"You can forget that from now on with your new sister in the house." "Everything is going to change, and you will need to be a big part of that help for your mother when she comes home tomorrow with Stephanie," he blurted out in his usual gruff voice, with Leanne remembering once again her friend who was forgotten once their baby came home. "We all have to make sacrifices, Leanne, and that includes you too, so you do as you're told and behave yourself. Help your mother, and be good to your sister or else," he bellowed as she ran to her room, resenting what was happening to her and how her life would change forever. She dared not to say anything to her father for fear that he would punish her again like he had done so many times in the past when her mother had gone out to her church meetings and she would be left alone with him.

Her bedroom closet was always so dark and scary when she was really bad and needed to be punished for things she didn't understand or even knew that she did wrong. The lock her father had put on the outside of her bedroom door kept her from escaping, so she lay huddled in her bed, praying that the monster her father convinced her was living in her closet would forgive her and not hurt her while she was trapped inside her room.

She recalled the many Sundays when she had been forced to go to church to learn about a God she was told to worship. She learned that He was a forgiving God and was always there to protect us so we never had to be afraid. She guessed that God didn't like her much, or why would He allow such bad things to happen to her that made her so afraid?

She had also learned about the devil, who had fallen to earth, discarded by God and heaven, and that made more sense to her. God didn't like him either. She considered that maybe if she loved the devil, who she felt was more like her, instead of God, she would be okay. She would have to be careful not to tell anyone and was convinced about what he could do for her when her sister came home.

Each time she was confined in her room, she

started to feel more and more comfortable with her devil, who had now become her friend, so much so that she eventually climbed into the closet for the love she needed and the protection he gave her. Nothing bad ever happened to her while she was inside, and with God never protecting her, she felt safe knowing that the devil was always there for her.

Her thoughts always raced while she was inside the closet with so much time to think about everything, and eventually, she believed that her new friend was guiding her to do things, feeling that he was the only one who truly loved and believed in her, and if she worked hard enough together with him, she could make this new sister suffer for everything happening in the house, instead of her. She would have *all* the control in this family, and she started to beam at the thought.

Her mother had always protected Leanne from her father's vicious temper knowing what he was capable of. Leanne thought carefully about her dad caring more about Stephanie than her, shuddering with the fear of what was to become of her now that her sister was taking away everything that she loved. Her mind raced as she prayed to her devil for help to destroy Stephanie.

While hearing Leanne mumble behind her closed door, Jean opened it and growled for her to "Go to sleep!" He couldn't stop thinking that this was simply too much work to do while he was so exhausted. "I am way too tired and have no time or patience for your foolishness tonight." "You're a big girl now, and your sister will be here after you wake up tomorrow."

She remembered him saying that things needed to change in their lives but wasn't quite sure what that meant for her. "What kind of things need to change, daddy?" Leanne asked, looking at him questioningly as he opened her bedroom door.

"Tomorrow, you can help me fix your bedroom to make room for the crib and rocking chair I have to buy for Stephanie." "You can help me pick them out too, but I forewarn you, I do not want any whining from you about buying toys when we are at the store!" "Now that we have another child to feed in this house, money will have to be used wisely, and we must make every penny count." "You will now have to take your toys to the basement. It will be your new place to play from now on," he commanded.

"But, Daddy, I don't want to play in the basement. It's cold and dark, and I want to stay in my bedroom like I do now with Mommy." "Why can't Stephanie stay down there instead?"

The childish suggestion made her father laugh out loud not thinking how a child would view what was happening or how she felt about the changes. He growled in his usual demanding voice, "No, that will never happen, so get used to it!" "Stephanie will not sleep through the night because babies don't do that, and she needs to be close to her mother so she can be fed often and cared for throughout the night and day."

Leanne thought for a moment and then wondered quietly to herself why they hated her so much. Then unthinkingly, she blurted out in a flash of panic, "But who will take care of me, Daddy?"

Without any care as to her feelings, he replied, "I told you that you are a big girl now, and you are too big to have Mommy baby you anymore." "You are five-years-old and a young lady now, and Mommy needs to spend all the time she can caring for Stephanie." You will be there every day for many years to come, helping your mother with housework, babysitting, and taking care of your little sister." "Now, I told you to go to sleep, and I will not tell you again! Tomorrow will be a big day for both of us." "You don't need a bedtime story, so get used to it before your mother sees how stupid you are being, and do not even try to bother your poor mother; she is exhausted and needs her rest." "She doesn't need the extra aggravation of you whining and crying over such silly things anymore, and I will be there to watch and make sure that it doesn't happen." "You will be punished if I find you disobeying me!" "Do you understand me?" he barked.

"Yes, Daddy," Leanne replied, hurt and ready to

cry at how this new baby was going to take her mother away from her and she would be left all alone to be forgotten. All she could think about was that she had to get rid of her sister as soon as possible. As her father closed the bedroom door, Leanne crawled into the closet with her devil friend, to plan her strategy for when her sister came home.

Many years would pass before Leanne would be seen for who and what she really was; a sinister monster with narcissistic, psychopathic, and sociopathic tendencies, which she had inherited from her father. She would do whatever was necessary to get what she wanted in life at any cost to those who got in her way. It would change the course of their family forever, and whoever was destroyed in the process was not important. It was the thrill of the hunt with the power to control and destroy that excited her. She was not only an intellectually gifted child but also truly cunning to its very definition and criminally sinister in her commitment to get what she wanted. She thrived on the terror she caused, undetected for years, with her main target always in her scope, Stephanie. She had many people convinced that she was sweet and innocent, but it was her plan all along, and she played it well. Should anyone cross her in some way, she would create a way to destroy that person without him or her ever seeing it coming.

When Leanne killed our mom for her money decades later, Stephanie worked emphatically to expose her, but Leanne's deceptive charisma, and evil cunning character prevailed once again, winning over those of any importance to her. They believed in her artificial Christianity and with her many years of drama lessons, together, they gave her the tools to get away with it. She was someone you couldn't stand up to without losing something of great value in your life. Those who were smart enough just backed off and stayed friends, supporting her for everything she wanted. If at any point Leanne felt duped or disrespected, those who tried would face serious retribution when they least expected it.

Stephanie refused to back off until it nearly cost her everything she loved; the most important people in her life, her job, her children, the alienation of her entire blood family, but most importantly, her own life. Stephanie never realized the extent of her sister's powers, but she would work harder in the years to come to expose her for what she truly was; a cunning, arrogant, and murderous bitch. Everyone had their weaknesses, but Leanne was pure evil like their dad, so it wasn't going to be an easy fight.

She would learn from Leanne that no one could be trusted, and that she was totally alone, but Stephanie wouldn't be defeated easily. Leanne would make her life a living hell any way she could, but Stephanie was born to fight, and survive, with a determination to win, or die trying.

CHAPTER 3

While most children fuss at taking a nap or going to bed at night, I remember the welcoming sensation that my little bed gave me each time I laid my head down, as far back as a year old. It was quiet and peaceful, and the walls that separated me from the sounds of fury and evil seemed far enough away that I felt safe within the bars that surrounded me. My bedroom was filled with my favorite stuffed animals. My name, Stephanie, was written across the wall in colorful block letters that in some way was intended to comfort me, but comfort was something that I never understood.

What did upset me was the darkness of the room that was forced upon me every night, and that horrifying rage from the other side of the wall where my parents slept. I was constantly threatened to be put into my bedroom closet, which was occupied by a hungry child-eating monster if I wasn't good, quiet, or compliant with my father's every command.

He actually enjoyed the story he told me about this monster that would devour my entire body slowly, loving the horrific pain he caused, while chewing his way through my bones. He would start at my feet, tearing me limb by limb while making his way to my head as I watched. The terror invaded my dreams and scared me to death during the day, fearing the monster might somehow escape and find me.

Night after night, I would awaken to the closet sounds in the room's total darkness, terrified that this monster in my closet could come out at any time. At such a young age, I had absolutely no understanding that our house was very old, and the pipes were responsible for making all the frightening noises I heard.

My father was relentless in making me believe in this beast, so I kept as quiet as I could while my heart pounded endlessly beneath my pajamas. I tried to think only of my mother's soothing tone and the childhood songs she would sing to me regularly, hoping that sleep would soon follow as it had done every other time she sang. This was not one of those soothing nights and hadn't been for a very long time. I lay perfectly still, hoping that the monster couldn't sense my fear. It was my father's favorite part of the story; sensing my fear before attacking.

After a few months, I eventually grew to accept the monster in my closet, who had never hurt me or caused any of the pain I was warned about, even when I was told I was being bad on a daily basis for no real reason. It was my sister, Leanne, who created the lies, convincing my father they were true. As strange as it was, the monster was becoming my friend, without ever seeing him or feeling any of the pain he had the ability to inflict. I started to believe that he actually liked me, so my fear of him gradually subsided.

Too frequently, I could hear the roar of the real monster, the one I could actually see, hear, feel, and truly feared behind the walls that separated our rooms. I would listen as he inflicted his grueling rage on my mother, ordering her not to listen to my cries when I called out for her to come, following the many nightmares I often had and forcing me to suffer the aftermath without her. I could hear her clearly as he tried to silence her with his threats and intimidation if she did. The anger rose just the same until I would hear my bedroom door swing open, revealing the shadow of him in the door frame from the hall light behind him. It was the shivering cold that followed him as he advanced toward me. The floor creaked as he got closer with only the glare from the nightlight across the room illuminating his demonic eyes with every step he took. The ominous fear rippled through my entire body with each step.

As my father hovered above me, I was terrified as to what he would do next and what would become of me. He had my face pushed heavily into my pillow, trying to silence my cries as I felt his heated breath on the back of my neck. He shouted at me in his gruff-like tone to shut up and stop my sniveling! Then came the evil grunts of laughter that followed, warning me in the same denouncing tone that my mother would never be coming to my rescue anymore and to go back to sleep right away, or he would release the closet beast!

My painful cries turned to silent whimpers as he kept pushing my head deeper into my pillow with his giant paw, making it difficult to breathe, and a grip too strong to resist. I lay very still, waiting for his grip to loosen with the hope that he would once again think he won and would soon leave.

As I lay quiet in total silence with him still standing over me, my body became lifeless. I pretended to fall back to sleep, terrified at what he would do if I didn't. No one ever challenged him in our house, and he thrived on the power and pain he inflicted on all of us. He loved the fear he saw in our eyes while satisfying his power and masochistic ego.

As his rage slowly lifted, so did the pressure on my head, and he walked slowly back toward the bedroom door, slamming it shut as hard as possible as he left to make a statement that he did not want to return for any other stupid childhood reason. The darkness of the room once again became inviting as I lay there quietly, afraid to move. My face felt hot from the pressure in the pillow, and my cheeks were stained from the tears rolling down my face.

After what seemed like a never-ending torment, afraid of being caught staring frightfully at him through the bars of my crib, I fell silent with my eyes still pressed tightly closed and finally went back to sleep as I was trained to do.

In the morning, when I woke, the sun was shining brightly through my window, replacing the darkness, and with it came the realization that the living nightmare was over once again for another night. The silence was serene and golden with the beautiful birds I loved to watch outside my window that would instantly calm me. I would wait anxiously for the door to re-open again; only this time, it would be my mother's smiling face, peering into my bedroom, as she did each morning, when it was safe to do so after dad left for work.

It was a cold February day, and I remember it because it was my first birthday. I was surrounded by so many people I didn't know. I learned later that they were my relatives. Dad was always different with his family present; he always had a smile on his lips, a joke at every opportunity, and a Canadian Club and gingerale in his hand.

The laughter while they were there was a happy time that we all enjoyed, and I wished they would never leave. It was a time that my mother referred to as a "family gathering," that we all looked forward to. There was no anger, no fear, no orders to jump at, and a sense of true happiness from the smile on everyone's faces that I learned to love and wanted more of. It was the only safe time for all of us.

Soon after everyone left, my mother would get me ready for our evening walk through the park that was close by. Although it was cold outside, it was always colder in the house when Dad was home with his intimidating gestures and evil that no one could escape from. We both enjoyed our time together, and there was always a feeling of being safe when Mom was near, especially when she held me in her arms before bed and he wasn't in the room to catch us.

Mom could always feel the discomfort before we left the house for our walk, so she would dress me up so toasty warm in a comfy blanket, removing me from the hell she knew we had to return to. We would start on our usual route, and I would smile, looking forward to the stroller ride she took me on. We would pass by the shop windows with the clothes she loved so much but could never afford.

I remember so well the yellow polka-dotted dress she used to stare at all the time whenever we passed by the shop window, not realizing at such a young age what it meant, but each time we passed, it would make her so happy. She would stand in front of me and pretend to dance wearing that dress. It was one of the rare times I saw her smile. That was the kind of person she was, always happy when we were alone and making me laugh at the simplest things around us.

We would continue our walk into the park behind the plaza onto this little wooden bridge with a stream running beneath it. The bridge made funny noises as the stroller rolled across it, and it was what I enjoyed so much. It made a strange rattle as we reached each wooden plank. I would watch the trickle of water below that I remember so well even though I was at an age I have been told was too young. Years later, we would talk about it as we both flashed back to the happy times in our lives that were very few, and the two of us loved to share.

I would always remember our walks with the most amazing woman I loved so dearly. She was the one who protected me against the giant beast who constantly tried to mold us both into his sadistic image. Leanne inherited his traits, so she loved the pain he caused and the control she was gaining from it. I was too busy being punished to understand, but he always won. This bastard would eventually take away my childhood at too young of an age. It was undeserved, unwanted, and unfair for any small child to experience, and it would also affect me for the rest of my life if I didn't learn how to overcome it, and survive.

CHAPTER 4

As time slowly came and went, the years passed, as we all learned our place within the family. We were poor, my father couldn't keep a job, and my mother worked hard to make ends meet. Grandma was now living with us and caused more problems than we needed. Dad couldn't stand her, usually because she was always so sick and took Mom's attention away from him. They were both strong-willed and constantly fighting over the most ridiculous things. It usually ended in a yelling match that echoed throughout the entire house with threats to throw her out. If it weren't for her and my mother running interference whenever possible, it would have been a lot worse. We were very poor but thankfully, both Mom and Grandma sewed, making the few clothes that we did have, though they were certainly not the stylish kind the other kids were wearing.

What Dad hated the most about Grandma was that she was old, feeble, and always whining about his dreadful behavior. She wasn't able to do anything more than babysit us kids and cook our meals. She couldn't leave the house because of her ailments so she was home the entire day, which meant that Dad's lies about going to a job he didn't have could easily be revealed. Now he would have to find somewhere to go after Mom went to work, and he hated her for it. He never knew it, but my sister's friends at school would often tell her that they saw him at the park feeding the ducks on their way home for lunch. Eventually, it got so bad that my father made mom put grandma into a nursing home several miles north of the city, where mom spent most of her weekends visiting her.

I tried my hardest to like my sister, but she was as sinister as my father in every respect. She would do something wrong and instantly blame it on me. Because she was five years older, and went out of her way to support him, my father loved her the most, and it was obvious. I wasn't the boy that my father always wanted, and he took his anger out on me whenever he could because of it. I could see how he watched the next-door neighbor's boy with his dad, throwing a baseball back and forth in their front yard. It was like a sparkle of true love they had in each other's eyes as they played together. I would notice the irritated expression on dad's face, but I hadn't known about my brother's death then, so I never understood what that look meant. I was way into my twenties when my mother finally told me about Peter, leaving out of course the specifics of his death, but it did explain a lot about what happened while I was growing up. I wanted more than anything to have my father love me, instead of his rejections and that devious smile on his face each time he punished me. I tried desperately to become the boy he wanted, with the fishing trips and other outdoor sports he persuaded me to do. I hated it all, but I did try my best to make him happy.

My sister, Leanne, would see what I was trying to do and would intercept by creating more problems I was somehow responsible for. She instantly blamed me for everything as if it were a competition she had to win, and she knew I didn't stand a chance. She gloated in the suffering she caused, so I spent most of my childhood in my bedroom with the monster in my closest. He became my only true friend in the world, and I called him "Bernie."

Leanne was exceptional in her own way. My father spent countless hours with her sitting outside in his car, where it was quiet, forcing her to study class work in order for her to excel in school. She never looked as though she hated it, but she never looked as though she liked it either. She knew that if it pleased dad, it would keep the peace between them and she would go undetected in the sinister and psychopathic chaos she created and blamed me for. She was a horrible human being, and it was clear that she inherited those traits from him, and copied him whenever possible, without hesitation.

The following year, my father surprised us all by bringing home a little black puppy. My mother wasn't too happy because of the extra cost we couldn't afford, but dad loved that little dog so much. He turned to us both and asked what we should call her. I wanted to call her Lassie after the television program, which we watched faithfully every time it came on the TV, and when it was clear enough to watch. We had terrible antennae reception, and the vertical lines constantly flowed through each program. Leanne would say that the dog looked as black as the night, so my father announced that her name would be Blackie. I cried as usual when she won everything because I knew that I meant nothing to him. I would just be sent to my room to cry so as not to upset everyone for being the "stupid little child" he always called me.

I knew I would be sent there anyway for questioning him or crying without a good reason. I would sit inside my closet, where I spent most of my time with Bernie, knowing I could trust him, that he would never hurt me, and he never did. I only heard him when the heat was turned on, but I was still too young to understand what that meant. Bernie became my only true friend. Then, the snake in the light fixture came to life above my bed, and the nightmares started once again. The light above me would flicker on and off, letting me know that the snake was angry, or so my father would tell me. I would cringe beneath the sheets each time it happened, fearful of him slithering his way down to my bed to devour me. Later, I would grow to understand that it was just the light bulb that was burning out and it flickered because it needed to be changed.

My mother wasn't allowed to comfort me at all while he was home, so she kept herself busy in the kitchen for reasons I couldn't understand at the time. It was only when my father left in the morning that I found comfort with my mother, who remained the wonderful loving woman she was, after he left the house.

CHAPTER 5

As time passed, my sister and I fought continuously and on a daily basis until my father started paying us twenty-five cents a day to keep out of the other's way. It kept us so distant at a time when sisters should be bonding like her friends had done with their siblings. I was never allowed to be around when her friends came to the house. They would tease and taunt me, making me feel as though I was not only unwanted by my family but also by everyone else. I felt rejected, alone, and always out of place. My only solace was in the food that I continuously stuffed into my mouth and hid from everyone.

Church on Sundays was always mandatory, whether we liked it or not. I was six years old when we were told we had to go to Sunday school with *no* exceptions. Leanne would make up headaches so she wouldn't have to go, but this day was different, and her intentional excuses didn't work. We were in the same class and learned all about heaven and how wonderful it was; with no family problems or diseases, hatred, mean tricks, and punishments. My days were filled with terror, and I always lived in fear of doing something wrong and being punished for them. Leanne watched from the corner of the room with her devilish smile, obviously working on her next plan to hurt me in some way.

I listened intently to the Sunday school teacher as we learned about this wonderful place. We had on our best clothes that Grandma had made for us and dad forced us to wear. Upon returning home from church, it was always dad's orders to change immediately before we were called down to lunch. As I went to my room to change, Leanne appeared at my bedroom door. She sat down on my bed with such a bizarre look on her face, reminding me of what we had learned about heaven. She was very polite for a change and less evil than on most other days.

She sat on my bed, reviewing with me what we had just learned. Then, turning to me, she started to tell me how I was the reason for our family having so many problems, and that if I wasn't so stupid and selfish, I could actually go to heaven sooner. There, I would be loved by everyone, always happy, and there would be no more punishments.

When I looked at her questioningly and asked why and how, she pulled a bottle of aspirin from her pocket and told me that if I took all of the pills inside the bottle, I could go to heaven now. I was only six years old and didn't quite understand how that could happen. It all sounded wonderful and a great way to end all of my problems. Then, she got up off my bed, kissed me on the cheek for the first time ever, and told me that mom and dad could finally be happy if I wasn't there to cause them anymore problems.

As she left my room, closing the door behind her, I thought about everything she had said, together with what the Sunday school teacher had told us about this great heaven place everyone wanted to go to, staring at the bottle. I reached over and took the bottle, which she had conveniently opened for me. There were so many pills, but I quickly ate them, trying not to choke as I swallowed. I lay silently on my bed as I did every Sunday, waiting for Mom to call, announcing lunch was ready, and then for the yelling to start, usually ending in a punishment I was somehow responsible for. I wondered how long it would take for these pills to take me to heaven and if God would come down on a white horse to take me there Himself.

It wasn't very long before I started to feel very sick to my stomach. I wanted to go downstairs to tell my mother, but I could hear the usual yelling start from the top of the stairs. I heard Leanne tell them that I was back causing problems again, that she had caught me in a lie and I was planning to come downstairs soon to tell more lies, just to get attention. My father became irate, yelling that he would not stand for anymore of my lies.

She told him that I was going to say that I took a bottle of pills, searching for the anger to rise up in his face that she loved so much to see. He roared in response, pounding his fist on the kitchen table, saying that he had had enough of me and how much trouble I would be in if I did such a thing. He screamed at my mother, ordering her to get his belt. I could hear my mother aggressively refusing and demanding him to stop, saying that maybe they should listen to me for once before reacting.

Still standing at the top of the stairs, I wasn't surprised as Leanne ran up quickly, pushing past me as she headed for my parents' bedroom, returning with the black belt he always used to threaten us with. She pushed past me, running back down the stairs with that demonic smile I hated, and I could hear my father praising her for being the only one in the damned house who would listen and comply with his orders.

I was terrified but at the same time becoming very sick from the pills, and I knew that my parents weren't going to believe that my dear sister would do such a terrible thing that could actually kill me. I went back to my bedroom, getting sicker by the minute. I was lying on my bed and wondering what to do as the vomit started to rise in my throat. On the TV commercials, we were always told in an emergency to call "0" on the phone. We didn't have 9-1-1 back in those days, so I ran across the hall to my parent's bedroom and picked up the phone. I dialed "0," and when the operator answered, I told her the entire story about heaven and my sister and the punishment I would get if I told anyone. She told me to go back to my bedroom and lie down, which I did when I heard the telephone start to ring. I lay there listening to my mother screaming at my father. Just then my bedroom door swung open, and my mother appeared in a hysterical state, dragging me to the bathroom to stick her fingers down my throat to make me vomit. It hadn't taken much of an effort at that point, but she made sure that I vomited everything that I could. She could see the pills that hadn't yet been digested, flying violently out of my mouth as she shook me vigorously afterwards, wondering why I would do such a thing.

She walked me back to my bedroom and held me closely as she lay beside me on the bed, telling me how much she loved me. I just lay silently in her arms, telling her that I was sorry and that I just wanted to go to heaven, where I wouldn't be a problem to anyone anymore. She sat weeping as my sister passed by my bedroom, listening intently, disgusted at her unsuccessful attempt to make me die. She knew then that she would have to be much more creative with her next attempt. My mother saved my life that day, and I became stronger for it.

CHAPTER 6

It was summer vacation from school for my sister and mom until the fall came, I would be starting kindergarten. I was excited at the thought but terrified at the same time, being told by my father that I would be away from my mother all day. He looked like he was smiling when he said it, and I didn't really understand what that meant.

Meanwhile, my sister would be home every day during the summer break. She would taunt and torture me the entire day when her friends came to play and participated in hurting me. I was so happy when my mother told me that my father would still go to work; that, at least, made me a little less frightened.

I stayed very close to my mother during the summer weeks, hoping she would see through my sister's facade and the hell that always followed. Mom was old school and an only child, so she never had sibling problems. She always claimed to be very lonely growing up, and that was the reason she wanted to have two or more children to happily grow through life together. She just tried to keep the peace with everyone at home, including the deranged man she married. She was easily manipulated by both; Leanne and dad, but somehow I knew that she loved me by the way she protected me from them when she could.

Although each day was very torturous, battling the constant conflicts with my sister by day and the punishments my father imposed on me at night, I could see how they prided themselves on their accomplishments, almost as if they planned it that way. If it weren't for Bernie being there for me, I would have totally lost my mind.

Dad would continue the private lessons with Leanne in his car every night and extra hours before summer vacation ended, prepping her for the year to come. Leanne was a star in my father's eyes, and it showed when she accelerated, skipping several grades throughout her school years. My father was so proud of her, but me, I was the bad seed who was hopeless and would not excel at anything. My mother noticed the favoritism, so she put more energy into me, or at least she tried.

Leanne was becoming more manipulative in her attempt to get me out of the family she worked so hard to build. When school started in the fall and I began kindergarten, I was afraid that I would never see my mom again when she dropped me off on the first day. I remember grabbing onto her leg, crying obsessively and refusing to let go.

On the night before I started school, my sister insisted to my parents that I had mental problems, that I was ruining the family, and that for everyone's sake, they should adopt me out to another family. As I listened intently from the top of the stairs, I could hear my parents agree that something needed to be done about me.

I went to school the next day, severely withdrawn. I backed myself into a corner at the opposite side of the classroom. I stayed there until my teacher approached me curiously to see what was going on, hoping that she could somehow comfort me. She was a wonderful lady and brought me lovingly to the front of the room during nap time. As we sat behind the spelling chart that protected us from being heard, I told her that my parents wanted to adopt me to another family. I was weeping uncontrollably as she took me in her arms and held me tight. I remember looking up at her with huge tears streaming down my face, begging her to take me home with her after school to be my new mommy, and promising to be a very good girl.

She looked as if she had no words for me, staring off into the distance while continuing to hold me tighter with a tear in her own eyes. She spoke reassuringly that I was such a wonderful little girl, while trying to consider the kind of hell I must be living in at home for me to say such a thing. She patted me on the back, sending me back to my mat to lie down, promising we would talk further once she went to the washroom. Her arms had felt so good around me, the same way my mother's arms had felt when she wasn't being told to stop by my dad. Reluctantly, I walked back to my mat with my eyes still wet from the tears that continued to flow down my face.

I lay there on my mat, weeping silently, hoping that she would come back and tell me that she would love to have me. Instead, she came back into the room several minutes later with my mother, whom she had called after she left, telling her that she had concerns about my home life, and that she would have to tell the principal about it. I heard my mother convince her to leave it with her, as she led me out of the school, and down the street to our house.

It was the first time I noticed the black cloud that hovered above our house and nowhere else on the street. I instinctively broke away from her grip and ran as fast as I could in the opposite direction from her and the evil I knew was there waiting for me. I was terrified, and she knew it. She ran after me and gently grabbed my arm. She pulled me toward her, holding me tight, and kissing my face. I knew then that she was aware of our family's evil dynamics and the terror that she too felt herself from her husband

and Leanne. As she crouched down beside me, she crossed her heart, promising me she would always be there for me and would do what she had to do to protect me. I believed the look on her face was genuine, but I knew in my own heart that she had no control over what happened in that house, and she was just as afraid as I was.

At the door, we were met by the devil we both feared. He was enraged that I would pull such a childish stunt and had been called by the school to deal with it, just to get attention. Mom sent me to my room while they argued. I could hear crashing on the floor as dad threw the dishes from the shelf that was within his reach, and for the first time, I was afraid he would hurt my mom. There was no end to what he was capable of, and it wouldn't be long before he would go too far.

I was so upset when I went to school the next day. I was mad at my teacher for calling my father. She tried to call me up to the front at nap time again, but I refused, telling her that she didn't understand anything about my family. I stayed quiet from then on, once again feeling rejected by another person. Now another hope in my life was crushed by someone I thought I could trust and had begged for help to rescue me. I became withdrawn and isolated myself from everything and everyone.

Gradually over the next few weeks, the tempers

in the house somewhat de-escalated, and we went back to the usual torturous days. As long as I was quiet and did what I was told, I was safe. My sister wallowed in the fighting that she had created but kept silent, waiting for the right moment to pounce again, suggesting to my father that they both go out to the car and study a subject at school she was having a problem with. She knew how to control him, and he thrived on the attention she gave him as her mentor and idol that would help destroy me.

Living such a lonely, rejected life hurt more than the punishments, but I forced myself to accept it. I wasn't allowed to use the house phone or to have any friends because I was told they were all bad influences on me. I was now eight years old. What kind of bad influences could they be? My sister, however, continued to flourish with dad's trust, and her friends were not only always welcome, but he would shower them with compliments, demanding why I couldn't be more like her. It was great for my sister because she knew she had dad where she wanted him, and she loved the degradation imposed on me in front of her friends. At school, I kept to myself, spent recess by myself, and I walked home from school myself, because no one liked me. They all considered me an unfriendly recluse, and made fun of me all the time with taunting remarks about the weight I gained.

CHAPTER 7

By the summer, when I was in grade 4, my mother convinced my father to allow me to go to day camp for a week. She would pay for it, and those were the magic words for him. I was so glad to get away from my sister that I jumped at the opportunity and actually smiled for once in my life. The camp bus would pick us up at my school and drop us off at the same place just up the street from the house. It seemed perfect for me until all the horror happened.

One morning into the week of camp in late August, there was a terrible fight at home just before I left for the bus. I ran out of the house but needed to go to the bathroom, number two, so badly, but I didn't have the nerve to go back home and be yelled at again for being so stupid. I just didn't have the strength to endure anymore pain for doing something I didn't do or couldn't control. Just the thought caused me to feel sick inside. I thought about going to a neighbor's house but that might have gotten back to my parents, so instead, I decided to knock on the school door, hoping that someone would answer and let me in. The bus would be there soon, and I would be in so much trouble if I missed it.

I was grateful when the janitor appeared within a few minutes. He had always been very nice to me, so I explained my problem, and he let me in. When I came out of the bathroom, he was lurking just outside the door waiting for me. I thought he was just being careful, having a student using the facilities on a day they were closed, so I thanked him for his help and started to leave for the bus when he said that he had something to show me. I couldn't understand what he could possibly want to show me, and I must have looked bewildered when he asked. He said that it was a puppy he had found on school property, and he wanted to know if I knew whom it belonged to. It made me feel so important that he would ask me of all people, so I agreed to go with him, as he ushered me into his janitorial closet. I looked at him confused when the door closed behind us and I couldn't see any puppy. He picked me up, put me onto his tool table, and told me to wait while he went to get it. Instead, he locked the door and turned to me while opening his pants, exposing his penis, which was as hard and as huge as a baseball bat. He came toward me and started rubbing it all over my chest through my clothes.

He told me that this was his puppy and that the puppy needed to be kissed as he tried to maneuver it toward my mouth. He rubbed it across my face to my lips as he pushed me down flat onto the table, dangling his penis over the top of my face, watching how terrified I was becoming and loving every minute.

I was terrified with what he was doing to me, but he kept telling me how beautiful I was and that it was something my parents paid him to do to me, and wanted me to learn. I started getting very scared because I didn't understand what was happening so fast. So many thoughts were running through my nine-year-old mind. He started to undo my pants, rubbing his penis between my legs with his gross and dirty hands. I tried to scream and run for the door as he laughed and told me that the door was locked and that my parents said I couldn't leave before I made him happy. I struggled with the door as he stood behind me, grabbing at my shirt, rubbing my undeveloped breasts, and trying desperately to take off my pants to get the sexual release he brought me there for.

Finally, I heard the bus driver blow his horn, telling the kids in the neighborhood that he was there and he wasn't willing to wait much longer. The janitor too heard the horn, and let me go because if I didn't show up for camp, they would call my parents wondering why I missed the bus. As I turned toward him, he had his penis in his hand rubbing it like a genie's lamp until so much junk came out of it, like water gushing from a fire hose. Looking down as he finished, he just smiled at me, grabbing me around the throat and warning me if I ever mentioned this to anyone that he would kill my family. Although that seemed like a good idea, he also said that he would tell my father that I refused to please him. That frightened me the most, so I promised not to tell anyone. I returned to the bus crying, trying to understand all of this in my mind and then having a really terrible day at camp. Again, I isolated myself from everyone around me, trying to understand why these bad things were happening to me, but I kept my promise and never mentioned it to anyone.

When school started in September, it was the janitor who opened the door for us every day. He was disgusting each time he looked at me, licking his lips and rubbing his crotch, while no one else could see him but me. Throughout the entire day, it was as if he was following me around because everywhere I turned, he was watching me.

I spent my days in class being quiet and keeping to myself, unable to concentrate on what my teachers were saying, so I did poorly in all my subjects. I would stare out the window, and he would be there. I would go to the bathroom in between classes, and he would follow me. He would be there waiting outside the bathroom door, making a motion with his hand slicing quickly across his throat, reminding me of the threat he had made in his room if I talked. It wasn't the motion that frightened me but the gurgling sound he made while doing it. I nearly tripped running back to my classroom, scared to death. I made a point of staying home from school sick for as long as I could.

I tried to play sick and stay home as much as possible, but I had already taken several weeks off and my grades were terrible. It was getting near the end of the school year and I was an emotional mess with the constant stalking, daily threats, and reminders of what he had done to me. I finally went home and told my parents the whole story of what happened that day at camp, leaving nothing out.

The worst part was that my father had been spending more alone time with me, calling it our "special time together," while mom volunteered at the church several nights a week. Dad was touching me like the janitor did, telling me how special and beautiful I was becoming. In my mind, that day at camp was coming back to me as vividly as it had that day, and I started to tremble. I tried to run to my bedroom with my father pulling me back onto the sofa with him.

Dad had always used a vibrator on what he called his aching bones, asking me to use it on the part of his back that he couldn't reach. The first time I helped him seemed genuine and innocent, but the next time he took the vibrator and put it between my legs, holding me down tightly within his grip, and telling me to wait for a couple of minutes until I felt it's effects; promising it would feel good, and I would love it. I couldn't move with his one leg over both of mine as he spread them apart, freezing me in the position he wanted.

I only had on my nightgown so there was nothing to protect me underneath except for the soft thin fabric that he had already lifted before the vibrator touched me, exposing my private parts that we had never talked about. I tried to fight him off the best I could, but he was overpowering and very determined to accomplish his task. His hold was hurting me so I stopped fighting, hoping it would all be over soon.

A few minutes passed before I started to feel that "good feeling" he talked about, just as he described. He was searching for what he wanted to see in my eyes, and made me look into his face with his one hand forcing me to look at him, as my body reacted.

I tried to break free from his grip, when his hand raced down to undo his pants, exposing his hard penis, and rubbing it frantically like the janitor had done during camp. As I groaned from the reaction that the vibrator gave me, the same junk gushed out of him like it had done with the janitor.

I knew then that telling my parents about the janitor was a mistake. I was confused if this was normal and the way life was supposed to be for a nine-year-old. When he finished himself off and his grip released, I ran upstairs to my bedroom, hoping to fall asleep as fast as I could.

When my mother returned later that night, she checked on me as she usually did. I was confused, scared, and didn't understand what had just happened to me or how I was feeling, so I said nothing to her. I was so happy to see her face as she opened my bedroom door with that loving smile that told me she was happy to see me.

She was so concerned with what I had told them earlier about the janitor that she insisted they would take me to the principal's office in the morning to deal with the situation. She promised that if I told the truth, everything would be okay. I was terrified but nodded apprehensively, feeling safe, knowing she was now home. I rested my head on my pillow until sleep took over seconds later. I slept until the morning when she woke me up.

I really didn't know what was about to happen in the principal's office, but she was insistent about us all being there, including my father. I shuddered at the thought, but I had no choice in the matter.

My parents sat quietly as I told the principal in detail what the bastard had done to me. She just scowled at me in disbelief and was outraged at my accusation, telling my parents that I had been a problem throughout the entire year, and she was convinced I was acting out for more attention at home. She was disgusted that I would lie about the janitor she herself had hired for the school, and that such an accusation would leave a permanent mark on his record.

On the way home, my father was abnormally quiet until we arrived and he sent me to my room. He quickly followed with his belt in hand to punish me for lying until my mother stepped in to prevent his attack. I was made to stay in my bedroom with no dinner that night, and as I lay in my closet with Bernie, away from the snake that could kill me, I found much comfort in being with Bernie, who I knew would protect me.

The school year was slowly coming to an end, and on the last day, my parents and I were called back into the principal's office. Once again, my father was furious at having to leave work again because of me, and angry about the money he would lose for another day off to deal with the problem. I remember seeing my father that night when he got the call from school with his belt dangling from his hand. Again, my mother took his attention away from me just before we left for the appointment, and saved me from another beating I didn't deserve.

This time, I was made to wait outside the principal's office while my parents quietly went in first, but I could hear clearly what everyone was saying. The principal took point in talking first, telling my parents that she had investigated the situation and again apologized for what had happened. Apparently, I was not the only little girl that the janitor had told about his lost puppy. There were five other little girl's parents who had come forward to complain about him for the same reason. She proceeded to tell my parents that the janitor had been fired for his indiscretions and breach of their school policy.

That seemed to satisfy my parents, and they took me home, telling me nothing of what the principal had said to them. There were no law-suit threats against the school and no arrest; he was just fired. There seemed to be no laws protecting children either against fathers who sexually abused their children, at least not any that I ever heard about. I was only nine-years-old, and I didn't know anything except the truth of what was happening to me. We went on with our lives with my father demanding that we never speak of it again.

CHAPTER 8

At the same time, I started having terrible chest and back pains. I was complaining about it to my parents almost daily. It was hard to breathe at times, but they brushed me off, thinking that it was just another ploy to get attention like what my sister was going through with her spine over the last several months.

Leanne got worse very quickly and underwent many tests until they discovered that she had something called scoliosis; curvature of the spine. It wasn't long before the surgeon stressed the importance of her having spinal surgery. He continued to say that it was very unusual for a child her age to have such a severe degree of deviation, and under different circumstances, he would normally recommend the patient wait until they turned twenty-one and stopped growing. Of course, with these extraordinary circumstances, the surgery date was set for the following month.

Leanne was hospitalized and underwent the

surgery that took over fifteen hours. It involved breaking her spine, stretching out the length of her curve, and then placing her on what they called a "Stryker Frame." The Stryker Frame consisted of two flat boards with a hole in the middle to go to the bathroom when needed. The board was attached to a huge wheel that would rotate her 180 degrees until it turned her completely onto another board. This was done every two hours. The trouble was that the boards were made for adults, and being as small as she was, when the wheel turned, she would sometimes slip out onto the floor. The surgery alone was horrific but then to actually fall onto the floor, sometimes daily, must have been unbearable. It wasn't that I enjoyed her pain, but I couldn't help but think that God was punishing her for all the torturing she had done to me for so long.

My parents were always at the hospital, trying to be positive while comforting her. Then they would come home exhausted and refused to acknowledge the same type of pain I was going through. I felt neglected, and everyone had convinced me that I was just having "sympathy pains." I was totally ignored and couldn't help but to cry out when my pains were contorting me into a ball of fire. I learned to hide it as much as I could, but it was really hard at times. Bernie seemed to be the only one I could talk to, and each time I did, I could hear the pipes crack and thought that it was Bernie trying to console me the only way I knew he could.

I stayed quiet for the entire six months until she was released from the hospital, hoping that the surgery might change her and she would be nicer toward me. It was a hope that gradually faded with each day she was home.

I tried very hard to forgive her for all the terrible things she had done to me, but honestly, it was an impossible task and something I knew I could never accomplish. In church, we learned to be a good person or God would punish us for our sins, and the last thing I needed were more punishments so I did try, hating every minute of it.

Leanne was restricted to bed rest, and I was told that we all had to do our duty to make her as comfortable as possible. Meanwhile, my pain was getting worse, and on a few occasions, I begged my mother to take me to the hospital to find out what was happening to me.

Finally, she gave in and took me, but the first thing out of her mouth to the emergency doctors was that my sister had just gone through hell with her spinal surgery. That was all the doctors needed to know, so instead of doing tests on me, they told my mother that it was all in my head and that if they gave me a little more attention at home, my pains would go away. I knew that this wasn't some sympathy crap

I was going through, and it wasn't going to get better with more attention. I resented the fact that they thought I was acting out because of some jealousy bullshit. I was in horrific pain, and the attention I wanted was for someone to help me.

Leanne did her part encouraging my parents to treat me like a nutcase, and they obliged in their own way, trying to keep her calm. Of course, Leanne was the intelligent child in the family, and I had every reason to be jealous of her, or so they thought. From then on, I just kept my mouth shut and sucked up the insufferable pain I was having. Too often, I could do nothing less than to yell out from the extreme pain on the football field at school and scream into my pillow when the pain woke me up from a sound sleep at night. I spent most of my time keeping out of Leanne's way when she was able to go back to school to finish her year with the usual honor status and help from dad.

I suffered for an entire year until the visible hump on my back got much worse, something like the Hunchback of Notre Dame. Clothes didn't fit me properly anymore, and the kids at school made fun of me. I was labeled a "freak," and it was so difficult to get through a day with the constricted breathing. I started skipping classes just so I could go home and lie down. Mom still worked days, which she was forced to do while Dad continued pretending he was close to getting another job and blaming me for losing the last job he never had with the janitor incident. The truth was that he lost all his jobs because of his offensive attitude toward others, and he was unable to work with anyone who didn't constantly complain about him. Every morning, he would leave the house, saying he was going to work and hoping not to be discovered for the monster he really was. My grandma would phone me from the nursing home, calling me names, and tired of my constant crying in pain, which she could hear on her end, but not once did she tell Mom about it, thinking this too would pass with time. She meant well, but she herself suffered terribly with pain, and I guessed that living in the back-woods alone toughened her up to the point that no one around her had the right to suffer aloud.

The kids at school started to tell me, as they did my sister, that their parents had seen Dad at the park feeding the ducks regularly when he should have been at work. This played a lot on my mind, helping me to understand that it wasn't my fault he was out of work all those times he made me feel guilty for getting him fired. Dad was mentally unstable, and now everyone else could see it too. I would just smile as I walked away in the opposite direction, satisfied, knowing what I heard was true.

My parents had no friends who called or came by to visit anymore, but my mother was still loved by everyone and was constantly invited out for luncheons behind my father's back. She must have known but never said anything until it was confirmed with the stories her friends told her about him. It just became a way of life for her, and she accepted it. The only thing that my father had going for him was the club meetings he attended. Somehow, they had made him president of the group, a job no one else wanted, so they put up with his narcissistic craziness.

The molestation continued for another two years with me growing more and more confused at what my father was doing to me. I was still unsure if it was acceptable for a father to do what he was doing to his own child, but I never said anything to anyone just in case. My pain continued to get worse each week until I got the idea to use it as an excuse to avoid him. I kept my distance and would just leave the room to go upstairs when I felt him advancing toward me, claiming I was feeling sick and needed to lie down. He was enraged at my rejection and began yelling verbal threats at me as I ran up to my room.

My father was becoming agitated at my refusals to his sexual advances, so he tried to make up for it by taking me out for ice cream every night when Mom and Leanne weren't home, telling me that it was our "little secret" and that I couldn't tell anyone, especially them. I wanted to agree because ice cream was a treat we rarely had, and it was one of my favorite foods. At the same time, I was thinking that maybe now my father might have actually changed after all this time and was learning to like me better. I didn't want to ruin the opportunity and thought carefully before answering him. I considered that we would be outside with lots of people around us so I at least had to try it once. As long as I made him happy without his sexual crap and I wasn't hunched over in pain, it just might be okay.

Things did start to get better in the house between us, and to my surprise, he actually growled at my sister once in awhile, as her pity trips finally stopped working. It only made her madder when my parents tuned out, but now he was in my corner, and it felt great to know that she couldn't get to me anymore without him scolding her for it. Leanne had become a bitch to everyone in the house, and I guessed that it was because of her surgery, or maybe my complaints about having so much pain that really pissed her off and made my father change toward her. She wasn't his sweet little princess anymore, and he made comments about it often.

I decided to go and see my family doctor, who I had been seeing privately for months about my weight gain. I found solace in eating with so much stress over the years, and the extra weight took its toll on my spine. The doctor prescribed diet pills to help me lose the weight but was far more concerned with the hump on my shoulder that needed to be diagnosed. He had been our family doctor since I was born, and when I finally told him about our family issues, except for the sex, he was totally shocked. I found it very hard to discuss that with anyone who mattered. I lived a very sheltered life and was never sure about anything that happened at home. I also had no way to differentiate the lies from the truth, the right from the wrong, and I was always too scared to ask.

The diet pills helped me a lot and made me feel great, as if I could deal with the everyday trouble in my life. With that courage, I would test the theory on my father somehow and thought hard about how I would do it. The doctor was now giving me pain pills to help with the pain along with the amphetamines, but the tests he would send me for would soon tell why my shoulder was protruding and the reason behind the horrific pain I was having. I was scared that I would have to prepare myself to face the worst possible scenario.

I tried to refuse the tests, telling him that my sister had just had spine surgery and there was so much going on in our house. He said he understood but was insistent on me having them done just the same, so I finally agreed. He gave me the requisition with an exclamation point on the top of the form, expressing its importance to the technicians, letting them know that the sooner they could get me in the better. I thanked him and left the office, terrified of what they would find but happy with the pain pills he claimed would help.

Between the amphetamines and the pain pills, I was able to filter the sexual abuse at home through the drugs, and it was working better than having nothing. I took the pain pills in the afternoon and before bed, while the amphetamines helped me get started in the morning. I was losing weight quickly, but it wasn't fast enough for me, and I wanted more. At dinnertime, my mom would force me to eat what she was serving, filled with grease and the carbohydrates I didn't want, so I would excuse myself to go to the bathroom and stick my fingers down my throat to throw up. Before I knew it, I was bulimic, using laxatives and living on celery stalks. Then I found an exercise machine on TV that would make me lose more weight. The "Slim Gym" was recommended for use twice daily for ten minutes. I used it four to five times a day for forty-five minutes, showing fabulous results. My life was starting to work in my favor as far as my weight was concerned, and how I saw myself in the mirror.

During the day, I could speed around like a jacked-up monkey, swinging from trees, and I felt that if anyone could catch me, then I wasn't moving fast enough. I would just have to move faster, and I did. I lost a lot more weight with the pills never leaving me to feel hungry, and the pain pills knocked me out at night. The excessive workouts were firming me up, and I was looking the best I ever had, and loving it.

After the janitor incident and my dad continuing to molest me, I could see him becoming more and more agitated when I started objecting to our "secret time" together that didn't include the ice cream treats. It was interfering with my new diet and exercising regime. Dad never knew about the medications, but I felt that he knew something was happening, affecting our diminishing sexual time together. He would confront me with threats, reminding me that our time together was not to be discussed with anyone and as his daughter; I was required to make him happy. I would just nod and leave the room, heading to my bedroom most of the time to get away from him. I would throw temper tantrums when he insisted that I come down to play when Mom went to church, and I could see how irritated it was making him. The more insistent he became, the more rebellious I was toward him.

CHAPTER 9

When I was twelve and just started junior high school, I met a girl named Sharon, who also had a rough life at home. She told me that she was being physically abused by her drunken father. We spent a lot of time together during school with us both showing up with bruises that no one cared enough about to question.

I finally told Sharon what was happening to me at home, and she surprised me by saying that molestation wasn't a normal thing for a father to do to his daughter. Yet, when I visited her at her apartment, her father was always home. He would greet me at the door, hugging me inappropriately, stinking of booze, and his hugging made me very uncomfortable. After studying, Sharon would still be in her bedroom when I left to go home. Her father would get up from his TV show, with his beer still in hand, and walk toward me saying that he would see me to the door. He was very polite and would tell me that it was always so good to see me. Then he would kiss me right on the lips, forcing his tongue into my mouth and cupping my breasts as his tongue probed deeper into my mouth, as if it were the normal way to say good-bye to someone. I hated it, but Sharon was the only friend I had, and I didn't want to lose her by telling her the truth about her dad.

When I got home that evening, I skipped dinner again with my father bringing to my attention that it was the third night in a row that I hadn't eaten. He was outraged that I didn't come right home after school when I knew my mother would be at church. He was hungry, claiming that she had forgotten to leave his food on the table, but I just shrugged my shoulders in response. He grabbed me and threw me into the kitchen so hard that I stumbled and fell to the floor. I crawled to the corner and cried while he stood over me with his face all contorted, disgusted by my disrespect. His eyes were clouded over and completely dead as if the lights were on and no one was home.

I knew what that meant, but after my conversation with Sharon, I was learning that what he wanted from me wasn't right, and I wasn't going to let it happen anymore. I slowly got up and told him that we needed to talk, but I never expected him to lash out and hit me across the face with a closed fist, yelling at me that I had no right to speak to him in that tone. The punch hit me so hard that I fell against the wall, crying out from the pain it caused and the cut now on my forehead trickling blood down to my chin.

He ordered me to make him his food with the sauce and spaghetti pasta already laid neatly out on the counter, demanding that I stop acting like a bitch. I was still whimpering but managed to start cooking his dinner, serving it to him exactly as he expected. I stood there while he took a bite, furious that I didn't do it properly. I cringed when he took his plate and threw it against the wall barely missing me, yelling that it wasn't good enough for even a dog to eat, and demanded that I clean up the mess before mom came home.

I knew then that it wasn't the food that made him mad; it was our "secret time" together he was so pissed off about. Before he left the kitchen, I blurted out that we wouldn't be doing those things anymore, and then, quickly mentioned that my girlfriend told me that it wasn't right. I left it at that and was glad I did.

The rage I saw in his eyes scared me worse than the punch to the face, and he hurled me again into the wall. Vomit started to swirl up into my throat as I tried desperately to get to the bathroom in time. I was almost there when he pulled me back by my hair from behind and then grabbed me around the throat, telling me that he would say when it was over. He screamed at me saying that if I had ever told anyone else again he would kill my mother and make my life the worst living hell I could ever imagine. He warned me that I was his daughter, his toy, and I should never forget it. "How much worse could he possibly make my life than the living hell it already was"? I just yelled back at him to go "screw himself," and the words shot out of my mouth before I realized what a mistake it was. I knew right then if I was going to survive, I would have to watch what I said to him in the future.

Afraid of his reaction, I cleaned up the spaghetti mess and the vomit and, then ran to my room to change my clothes before going to bed, praying for the sleep I was unable to have the past several nights. As I went to remove my clothes, the door swung open, and he stood there with his dead eyes and angry scowl, ordering me to take the rest of my clothes off nice and slow as he watched. I just stood there frightened until somewhere inside of me blurted out that this was enough, and I slammed the door in his face, catching his hand in the door frame and screaming for him to go away. Before he had a chance to retaliate, the front door opened with my mother returning from church with her usual smiling face and happy tone calling out "Hello, everyone, I'm home."

CHAPTER 10

Dad quickly walked down the hall to greet her with a smile as if nothing had happened. I could hear him say that they had a serious problem with me and that something needed to be done right away. My mother knew that I had become very depressed since the janitor incident, but she still wasn't aware of anything happening between my father and me while she was gone. I fought to hear what they were saying from the stairs, but they had moved into the kitchen far enough away that I was unable to hear.

I lay in bed under the covers when my mother came up to kiss me good night, opening my door, anxious to hear about my day. She had been crying, and that was clear. She told me that they were both very concerned with my behavior and depression, and that my father had suggested something that she had finally agreed to. Within a few minutes of us talking, he appeared in the hallway behind her with his coat on and my jacket in his hand, telling me to get dressed, and to get into the car.

"We're going for a drive!" he shouted as my mother helped me up, not yet noticing the bruise that was slowly forming on my face and neck, and the fresh cut on my face that dad said I had done to myself.

Dad forcibly grabbed my hand and dragged me to the car as we drove toward the hospital, warning me to behave and to keep silent or things would get a lot worse for me, as if that were even possible. As we sat in the ER waiting room, I asked him what was happening and asked if he was sick, wondering why we were there. He never replied, and when his name was called, he told me to stay where I was put until he motioned for me to come forward. We were joined by two large men in white coats who took both my arms, making it impossible to break away from their grasp. All my father could say as they led me away was that it was for my own good.

As I turned to look over my shoulder, I saw my father walking briskly toward the exit door as these two men escorted me onto the elevator and pushed the seventh-floor button. It was strange because they needed to select a specific code to get to the floor and another code once we arrived that I didn't understand. We were greeted by a nurse who lovingly took me from their grasp and led me to a private room with only a bed and a dresser in it. As I viewed the entire room, I could see that the bed and dresser were bolted to the floor. The nurse turned to me and told me to take off all my clothes and put on the gown that was left there for me on the bed. As she was closing the door, she told me that in the morning, I would see the doctor. My door actually locked behind her and I was trapped. I still didn't understand anything that was going on and yelled out to her, asking if this was about my back. I felt like a wild animal thrown into a concrete cage with only a barred window on the door to be watched by those who walked by, starring in at me as if I were about to do some kind of trick. All I could do was hide my head and cry.

The next day, my door was released by another nurse standing before me with a breakfast tray, telling me that I had five minutes to eat before my appointment with the doctor. I was hungry and wolfed the food down quickly with no problem. I couldn't remember the last time I had eaten, but wearing this disgusting gown made me realize just how much weight I had lost.

The doctor was really nice to me as I entered his office and saw him open up a file. He motioned for me to sit in the chair opposite him and then asked me about the terrible bruises that had developed on my face. He asked me if I knew why I was there, and I could only shake my head. He continued on to say that my parents were worried about me and my unacceptable behavior at home and then asked me to explain. My gown, which was too big for me, shifted slightly to show the bruising around my neck.

When asked about the bruises, I considered the question and then shook my head, afraid to tell anyone or suffer the consequences I was warned about if I did. I was sent back to my room under lock and key after our visit, noticing the elevator again and the key code that was necessary when anyone came or left the floor. I ate my food when it arrived at lunch and was generally a very nice and polite child when I wasn't being abused at home. That seemed to confuse those who mattered, and the same nurse who escorted me to and from my appointments told me what a very sweet girl I was, looking confused as she spoke and wondering why I was there. I wasn't the usual depraved patient she was used to seeing on the floor and as she locked the door behind her, she continued staring at me through the barred window that separated us until I smiled and waved to her in an innocent fashion, thanking her again for the food.

Two weeks had passed, the bruises had healed, and I was regaining the weight I had lost starving myself, hoping to die, thinking that it was my only way out of this life. My doctor was very satisfied with my progress and asked me again if I knew why I was there. I shook my head again, afraid to speak. He proceeded to tell me that I was brought in for being something they called a pathological liar with ODD tendencies (oppositional defiant disorder). He explained to me that a pathological liar was someone who believed in the lies he or she told, and the ODD was when someone was severely rebellious against parents and/or authority figures, which explained the serious problems at home. Apparently, my father had convinced him that our home life was so bad that they were frightened I may kill them if something wasn't done immediately. I was shocked and could only shake my head with disbelief that a doctor of his status could believe such a bullshit story. I did hand it to my father though for coming up with such a demonic ruse to protect him and could only hope that my doctor was smart enough to see through his evil masquerade. Now the game was on, and if I didn't want to spend the rest of my life in a mental institution, I would have to tell my side of the story, and soon.

I could only look at him bewildered and tell him that we had learned in church that lying was not acceptable if you wanted to go to heaven, and that I never lied or I would get punished severely by God, or worse, by my father. Before continuing, I remembered my father warning me not to tell anyone about our "secret time," or he would kill my mother. I loved her too much to do that, so I stopped in mid-sentence. He noticed my hesitation and tried to get me to continue, but I just stayed silent, looking into the distance with a blank expression. It was as if he knew what I was about to say and the truth of why I was there. It would take time and trust to break through to that truth, but he was determined to find it.

After a few more appointments, he hoped that he had built a strong enough trust between us to ask me again about the bruises he found when we first met. He was always so nice and kept telling me that whatever I said in his office would never go any further than the room, including my parents. I wasn't sure if it was a trick, and I certainly didn't want my mother killed because I was too stupid by running my mouth off with the truth. I did like him a lot and felt very comfortable talking to him. I just responded with a blank expression and then asked him if he promised. It was as if a light had gone off in his head, and he nodded convincingly.

I was sitting on his sofa at the time, and when he came out from behind his desk to sit beside me, I crossed my legs and folded my arms across my chest to protect myself in case he would touch me like the other men had done. As he sat down, I moved to the other side of the sofa, and he noticed it right away. He reached his hand toward my arm while trying to comfort me, observing what his professional suspicions were telling him.

He looked me straight in the eye and told me that he was there to protect me from anything in my life that frightened me. It was the expression on his face that I liked and felt so comfortable with that I started to say what was on my mind; my fears, my home life, my teacher's rejection, Bernie, the snake, my pain, the solitude I constantly battled, the janitor, and finally my dad. As I spilled my guts, I couldn't stop the trembling in my body and uncontrollable tears that raced down my cheeks. It was as if a huge weight had been lifted from me, and I could see a tear in his own eyes as I told him the whole sordid story. I couldn't stop, and it felt great to get everything out of me even if it was blurted out in one long sentence. It was such a relief to finally tell someone I could trust, but I made him promise again not to tell my dad or mom.

He became very disturbed at what he heard, yet his words continued to be calm and comforting as he explained that I was due to be released, and would be going home later that day. As he watched my entire body twitch at the thought, he quickly injected that he wasn't going to allow that to happen, after finally hearing the truth. It was the certainty in his voice that told me he actually believed me and cared, something that I wasn't used to. He continued to tell me that what had happened to me was not right in any way, that it wasn't my fault, and I was what they called a "victim."

He was confident in telling me that I did have an option, so I listened intently. I could remain a victim, or I could learn to find the strength within myself to become a "survivor." Everything was happening so fast, but I was pleased with his promise not to tell a soul about our sessions. He went on to say that there was another choice he thought would work for me because of my age, and that was to place me in a home for "juvenile delinquents." I wasn't exactly sure what that meant, but if I agreed, he would take me there the next morning. Naturally, I agreed without hesitation.

The following day, my doctor took me to the home he spoke of. It was like a jail or what my interpretation of a jail would be at my age, having watched the news with my parents every night. The kids were callous and mean, and the boys looked at me like my father always did, and I was terrified.

It was lunchtime when we arrived, and suddenly, two disturbed boys started throwing food at each other. One of them stood up with what looked like a toothbrush with a blade taped to the end of it in his hand and slashed the other boy across the neck. The gash spewed out blood in every direction. He fell to the floor, contorted with the pain and losing so much blood. I ran for the door, but it was locked, so I scrambled furiously to free myself from the other kids pawing their way to escape this dungeon any way that I could. It was a frantic, bloody scene that I wanted no part of, and I was scared to death that I would be the next to die.

The adrenalin was rapidly flowing inside me as my doctor fought his way toward me. He grabbed me from behind, holding my arms tightly to my side and frightening me to death, but as he turned me around, I could see who it was, and I grabbed onto him for dear life, screaming at him to take me back to the hospital. There was no way that I would ever live in such a place; and would rather be back home than in there. He saw it written all over my face and assured me that I was safe and he would take me back to the hospital. I was so overcome with fear that I dropped to the floor and passed out, waking up in the emergency room, shaking hysterically and fighting anyone who tried to touch me.

I could see my doctor running toward me from the nursing station, ordering the nurse to bring a syringe to sedate me. He sat beside me as the drug began to work, his brow furrowed and hung low with his hand clasped in mine as he recalled the devastating situation he had just put me through, worried that I might not recover from it. He spoke in that calming voice I loved so much as I stared into the distance while the drug took over my mind. The last thing I remember saying before falling asleep, was, "I guess this is my life."

We returned to the psychiatric floor, and I was put back into my room. The doctor came in a few minutes later, still covered in the blood from the boy, which got on his shirt and tie when he tried to resuscitate him and failed. The boy had died from the attack, and I was grateful that I survived. He took off his tie and put on his white jacket to try to hide the blood, but seeing it started to freak me out again. I was still frantic when he gave my nurse the order to up the sedation dosage. The nurse ran in with a syringe and gave me another shot before I knew what was happening and could react. Within minutes, I was calm, lying on my bed intoxicated by the drug, which sent me into such a relaxed state that I wasn't used to. I began looking back on my life with everything that had happened to me over the years.

I thought about my sister, her attempts to destroy me, and my father's punishments. I also thought about all the times she spent in his car when no one else was allowed, and it made a lot of sense to me that he had done something to her as well, and that was the reason she was so mean toward me.

I still had so much resentment for them both, but I did what I thought I could do at the time to keep the peace and make everyone happy. If it wasn't for mom begging me to try, I wouldn't have put so much effort into it. I had become very rebellious and oppositional only because I knew that I couldn't trust either of them, and my life could drastically change for the worst with anything that I said or did. At the drop of a hat, I would suffer if I wasn't careful, so I totally withdrew further inside myself. I remember so clearly when Leanne convinced my parents to adopt me out, recalling the conversation as if it had just happened. The doctor called it PTSD, but I had no clue what that meant.

I was almost eleven and wished that my life would end. I missed my birthday being in the hospital. No one came to see me, no cake, no gifts, and not even a card to wish me a happy day. I assumed it was something ordered by my father, but I was never sure. I thought my mother would at least come and be there for me, but I knew she was afraid of Dad too and wouldn't disobey his orders. Having my birthday forgotten wasn't out of the ordinary. My birthday always came soon after Christmas and probably was also an expense they couldn't afford. Christmas wasn't a fun time either when both my sister and I received only one gift each. The gifts were identical so as not to cause any problems between us, but she was five years older and we had different wants, needs, and interests. I always lost then too with her getting what she wanted. I had to be happy with the same thing or it was taken away from me. One year, they bought us both dolls. While she was thrilled, I took a pen and gouged out my doll's eyes. To this day, decades later, I still have that doll in my mother's hope chest. At least now, my parents had a good excuse to forget my birthday again.

I was still in the hospital, still friendless, a total recluse, and I woke up every day hoping that when I did get out, I would be killed by a car or a bus trying to cross the street. It would at least end my suffering or so I hoped. My mind had been destroyed by those I trusted, and I just didn't care anymore.

The doctor came in the next day to see me in my room instead of his office, surprising me with my mother there to take me home. He had already spoken to her about my physical abuse, and from her reaction, I don't think he told her about the sexual stuff. After all, he had promised to protect me and now he hoped to never see me there again unless it was of my choice. I felt safe in my little concrete cell, and everyone was so nice to me. I was sad in a way that I had to leave and go home to the hell that terrified me.

My mother, who I thought was innocent about everything, convinced the doctor to give our family another chance. She promised him that things would change at home, and they wouldn't give me any reason to make up more stories. She obviously wasn't listening to the doctor, but that was Mom. She must have been very convincing because the doctor believed her and decided to release me into her care.

There were responsibilities attached, and I listened to him ramble them off to her. He was explicit that he did not want me exposed to anymore of my Dad and Leanne's indiscretions, the constant taunting and punishments, or being left alone with either of them at any time without her present. Although my mother wasn't quite sure exactly what he was referring to, she agreed without hesitation and promised him while crossing her heart.

All the beds on the ward were filled now, and they needed my room for new patients. Because there was no actual proof that my father had really done anything to me and the bruises could have been self-inflicted, he had no choice but to let her take me home.

CHAPTER 11

As we walked out of the ward, Mom promised me that she would never leave me alone, and she would quit the church to be closer to me. She went on to say that she and dad had talked everyday for the past several weeks, regretting that they had sent me to the psych ward. She held me tight, telling me how much she loved me and that she would always be there for me. She was good at convincing me too, and I believed every word she spoke, except about my father. I could only hold her tight and plead with her to please keep her promise. She just looked at me questioningly, but mom was very prudish and would have denied any truth with what dad had done to me.

When I arrived at home, they had a welcome-home cake for me, and everything in the past that happened seemed to just be a bad nightmare. I could tell that my father was trying to be very good to me, which made me very uneasy, anticipating his next attack. My mother made all my favorite foods, thinking that it would make up for everything that had happened. After dinner, my father came back into the kitchen and told me that he was sorry for what I thought had happened, and he would give me some space to have friends if I promised not to get into any further trouble. I understood perfectly what that meant and was always on my guard when we were alone together. Then, like a sharp muscle spasm, it shot out of his mouth like vomit from food poisoning, demanding to know what I was going to do about school; concerned that I wouldn't pass. He suggested that we do what he had done for my sister by studying in the car each night, where he claimed it was quieter with no distractions. I just agreed that we could start once I went back to my classes first, to see if I could catch up on my own, and surprisingly, he agreed.

His controlling attitude was a part of who he was, so I knew he couldn't help himself. He was still the worst monster a person could ever imagine, but if I had to live there, I would at least have to accept that part of him. The rest I would just avoid at any cost, usually making myself unavailable when I knew we would be home alone together.

Junior high would be much more difficult academically than grade school. With the year almost over, it would take a lot of effort to get caught up. The gossip somehow quickly traveled throughout the entire school about me being in the psych ward. The kids were cruel and teased me about it daily, making it terribly hard to ignore them in the halls as they laughed and pointed at me. There was no doubt in my mind that Leanne was responsible for the rumors.

The stress, combined with the amount of work needed to catch up was nothing compared to the inflating trouble at home, which made it impossible to commit to my school-work. I promised to do my best with the few days left to do it in, and I tried really hard, until I couldn't.

Trouble gradually became much worse again at home as if I wasn't supposed to notice. Knowing the bastard as well as I did, I assumed that it was probably his plan from the day I got home. You always had to be one step ahead of his evil, which meant that I needed to be on guard for every little thing, and at any given time of the day or night.

My mother never did leave the church, and I was starting to understand why, but I made sure that I hung out with the odd friend I could get, just to keep away from him, and the secret times he insisted having again. It compromised my ability to study, and I was so far behind that I knew passing was not going to happen. Of course, spending more time with any type of friends would inevitably get me into trouble somehow, but I just didn't care anymore.

It was the early seventy's when pot and hashish

were becoming very prominent at school. Everyone was doing it, so I took whatever friendships I could get, hoping that I wouldn't get caught. My friend Kelly invited me to Raj's place on evenings when his dad was at work. Raj was the local drug dealer. He was two grades ahead of us, but it was an outlet for me just the same, and I needed it badly. Unknown to me at the time, we weren't just asked to his place to party, but to help him cut up the kilos of the hash he was selling to kids at school. These were the "coolest kids" and I felt as though I was part of an elite group that the rest of the school looked up to. I was excited that they had asked me to join them, but I really didn't know what hashish was, so when the joint was passed around, I wasn't going to be the only one there who didn't accept it.

I recognized a few kids from my classes who also came and who up to then had hated me for being what they called a "total loser." They gawked at me upon arrival as if I were a "snitch" and wondered why I was even invited. Kelly assured them that I was cool, so they continued to weigh this brown tar-like stuff, while I sat on the living room floor working hard to be accepted.

I had never done any street drugs voluntarily so after a few puffs of the joint, I could feel the effects. At first, I felt nauseated and then very hungry. I remember Raj saying that he had added something called opium oil to the joints, and that was probably the reason I found myself sitting in a corner hallucinating, a little paranoid about the kids I was with, and my mind wandering to so many negative things, just wanting to go home.

Johnny, a popular boy from my class, soon arrived. His father was a teacher at our school, and Johnny was so gorgeous that I used to dream about him being my boyfriend from the time we met in class on the first day of school. I knew very well that I never had a chance with him and saw him with a different beautiful girl several times a week. He soon noticed me and after a short time convinced me to go into the bedroom where it was quiet and we could talk, promising he would take care of me.

I must have fallen asleep because when I woke up, my panties were off and my private parts hurt. I had been a virgin up until then, but now there was blood on the sheets and he was lying beside me in a cold sweat with his pants off and a smile on his face. The sleep had sobered me up, and as I got up, I reached for a towel close by and wiped the blood off before dressing. When I looked at the clock, I saw that it was well after midnight and past my curfew. I was going to be in big trouble when I got home, so I rushed out the door without an explanation with everyone staring, and shaking their heads as the door slammed behind me.

As I sneaked carefully in our front door, I was relieved that my parents were in bed fast asleep. I crept quietly up the stairs to my bedroom and crawled into bed, elated that I was able to get away with being late and thinking that I had had sex for the first time with someone who actually loved me. After all, it was my impression that only people in love had sex. I fell asleep with a smile on my face and drifted off into sweet dreams about this man who claimed to love me and wanted me forever.

The next day at school, Johnny just ignored me as if nothing had happened. I found him in the hall before class flirting with another girl, but I really needed to talk to him about what we had done, happy that now we would be together and maybe even live together, rescuing me from the life I hated. I was shocked when he told me that it was just sex and he would "see me around sometime." I left my classes early, wondering what had just happened. I went home and cried in my room, wanting to die and thinking that my only hope for happiness had just been blown to hell.

The school year ended with me unable to catch up and lying to my dad about my marks. I had missed too much school and held my father responsible for it when he committed me in the hospital. The school gave me the option to catch up at summer school, but with all the drama at home, I knew it wasn't going to happen. It meant long hours in the house studying with my father constantly looking over my shoulder. The sexual advances were progressing with him trying to convince me that the touching was purely innocent when I knew that it was inappropriate. I managed to speak to all of my teachers, explaining that I had been in the hospital, and if they would just pass me, I promised I would do better in grade 8. When they denied my request, I went home and lied to my father, telling him that I passed the year with good grades. When he asked for my report card, I told him it was in my back-pack and someone had stolen it out of my locker. He was furious, but I promised when school started back I would get him another copy. That would at least buy me some time to think, and it seemed to satisfy him.

Before going to the hospital, I had met a girl down the street named Donna. She was wild and crazy, but I really liked her, so I hid her from my parents until she got me into trouble smoking cigarettes in the underground parking garage where she lived. She was devious and really good at it, telling me all about her father and his sexual exploits with her as well. I listened intently without mentioning anything about my father, but I liked her a lot so I did what she told me to do to avoid losing her friendship.

I was actually ten when I started smoking cigarettes periodically. They were fifty-one cents a pack and sold at any pharmacy. They would accept a note from either parent so kids could buy smokes for them. I became very good at forging my mother's signature and the pharmacy never checked.

Donna and I would go to the underground parking garage and smoke an entire pack of twenty cigarettes before going home. There was nowhere to hide the rest of the package at home so we had no choice but to smoke the entire pack. Sometimes, she insisted that we skip the last class of the day with another forged note from our parents, allowing for us to leave for a doctor's appointment we didn't have, and then head to the garage again. I would rifle through my father's pockets the night before for change to buy another pack, and he never let on that he noticed. For sure, he would have said something if he did.

Unfortunately, but not surprisingly, Donna was also a kleptomaniac, and I noticed it right away each time she took me to the pharmacy. She talked me into doing the same thing, stealing small things at first, like gum. She was so good at it that we would go into other stores in the mall and steal clothes that we would try on and wear under our own clothes while we walked out of the store. It was like a victory; getting away with something that I actually did for once, and it made me feel good. It became a habit until I got home one day, and my father had noticed all the really cool clothes in my closet he knew that we couldn't afford and asked me where they came from. All I could think to say was that I borrowed them from my new friend Donna. It was a pretty simple lie until they tracked down her parents and found out the truth. I was grounded for a month and was never allowed to see her again.

My friend Sharon called me one night soon after my hospital experience, asking to get together. I insisted we meet somewhere other than her apartment, mostly because of her father, who was always home and another encounter I wanted to avoid. We both decided it was time to take our relationship to the next level by going out drinking at downtown bars. I was vulnerable, but I always did what I was told to do so as not to suffer any punishment. My grounding was finally over, and it was the perfect opportunity to have some fun again.

Drinking had never been my thing, but I would finish what was left in the glasses at family gatherings. I managed to borrow a girl's ID when she left her purse on the bathroom counter at the mall one day before going into the stall. That got me into every bar without a problem, so, we began sneaking out of the house when our parents went to bed on weekends. We were having the time of our lives meeting guys, dancing, and drinking wonderful drinks that made me feel great. I finally found an outlet for my misery, and it was alcohol.

Then, one night after having a great time, I got caught by my father who was hiding in the shadows of the hall as I sneaked through the front door. Every other time was great, and it gave me a sense of accomplishment, but I guessed that he finally caught onto me. He was outraged that I had once again defied him, and as we shouted at each other, he ripped the telephone cord out of the wall and wrapped it around my neck. My mother stood at the top of the stairs, yelling frantically at him to stop or he would kill me. He panicked, probably for the first time in his life, and listened to her as he released the cord.

CHAPTER 12

Leanne was now going on sixteen and she was off to university in the fall after skipping a few grades. She would be one of the youngest university students there and loved the attention. She was privileged, being the only child in our family who was given the opportunity that I had no chance of ever having. My grades were low only because of the hell I endured during public school; being constantly rejected by my family each day, the endless fighting, resisting dad's sexual advances, and never learning how to win. My education was totally ruined by these monsters, regardless of the tremendous effort I made to simply survive. The day I heard Leanne was moving out of the house, I could see a light at the end of this dark tunnel with one less monster to fear and fight, or so I thought.

I had never known such peace until Leanne moved out. The fall and winter were almost perfect, with the exception of my father and his usual molestation attempts, but with the pain in my back each day, and the meds the doctor gave me, I was able to maintain a minimal amount of sanity keeping away from him.

Now, with spring quickly approaching, my sister popped by the house unexpectedly to visit me without my parents knowing. She was unusually kind to me and apologized for everything she had done. She went on to say that it was just "sibling rivalry" and begged for my forgiveness, which I reluctantly gave, with the hope that things between us might possibly get better. What a mistake!

We actually hugged for the first time in our lives, but I was still skeptical when she stopped by again, the following day. She came to invite me to an upcoming frat party at her university co-op dorm. I agreed to go with her, and my parents actually gave me permission to stay overnight because they trusted her to take care of me. I would jump at any opportunity to get out of the house and at least try to develop a better relationship with her.

Dressed in makeup, silk stockings, and an awesome outfit Donna had given me, I arrived at her dorm with her saying how glad she was that I had come. I polished up my makeup before we made our way down the hall, feeling good about the way I looked. She introduced me to everyone as her awesome sister, and they seemed genuinely interested in meeting me. At that time, Leanne and I could pass ourselves off as twins, because we looked so much alike even though we were five years apart. The guys would shower me with compliments, hugging and kissing me as we met. It was something I had never felt before. Leanne had never told anyone her actual age, so they just assumed, being her twin, I too was of an age to party, and not the jail-bait I actually was.

Soon after, my sister disappeared, and I was alone with all these partying university men, pouring alcohol and drugs into my mouth without much of a fight from me. I had never felt as alive as I did that night. When it got very late, I was still having a fabulous time alone with these guys doting on me, but I was getting really stoned from whatever they had given me, and I knew it was time to go back to Leanne's room. I fought to walk down the hall, and as I was trying to open her door, I found it was locked and she didn't answer when I called out her name.

I was stumbling along back down the hall trying to find her when five great-looking guys pulled me into their room, smiling and obviously drunk, having a great time. It just seemed too convenient for them to be there at that exact time I was, but I was thankful that I had somewhere to go and rest safely until my sister got back to her room. I was too wasted to even think of trying to find a bus to go home. It was a huge campus, very late, and I didn't know if the buses were even running at all.

As the guys led me into their room, another beer appeared in my hand, while another was poured down my throat to help me swallow the additional pills they laughingly put into my mouth. As the beer started to spill all over my outfit, a third guy told me that I couldn't go home smelling like a brewery and proceeded to take my dress off while another held my arms up over my head. The blonde guy told me that I should lie down and just enjoy the stone I was about to have. I was already feeling the effects from the first drugs given to me down the hall, which I normally wouldn't have accepted, but they told me that my sister had wanted me to have a memorable time, and they promised her they would make that happen.

I was becoming very uncomfortable with what they were doing to me and told them that I needed to go back to my sister's room, or I would be in trouble. The one pouring the drugs and beer down my throat told me that they had already cleared it with her, and she had given her permission for them to keep me all night, as long as they had me back by seven in the morning. Apparently, Leanne was called away on an emergency and wouldn't be back until then.

My mind and body were becoming very numb as the drugs and booze took effect. I still had the presence of mind to realize that something was very wrong with this whole situation, and felt my sister's evil hand all over it. She had almost gained my trust over the past few months since she moved out of the house, and I was pleased with the closeness that was developing between us, until now. It would soon be clear that the bitch had set me up to suffer what was about to happen, and within minutes, my body was completely lifeless and I was unable to move at all.

There were the six of us in the room, five men and me, just a few doors down the hall from her room. They told me that she would join our party as soon as she could, but how could she do that if she wouldn't be back until morning? It didn't make any sense. My body lay limp as they laid me down on the bed, now totally naked. Somehow, my bra and panties had also been removed, but I was too numb to fight. I was still cognitive of what was happening, even with the drugs and alcohol I was given, but I just couldn't control my body or even struggle. I lay there, watching as these five men took off their clothes, telling me that it was time we all went to sleep. They kept repeating they would take very good care of me, giving me the best pleasure I could ever imagine. I wasn't quite sure what that meant with my head in such a fog, and my body totally motionless. I didn't understand what was about to happen to me until it started, and with no way to make it stop. I could only hope that I would survive what they had in store for me.

It wasn't long before the dark-haired man was pushing another pill and more alcohol into my mouth. I was lying naked and spread-eagle on the bed while the other four carefully turned me over onto my stomach, strategically positioning me on top of him. I still couldn't budge, and things were happening too fast. My body was limp, and I was unable to fight them off. I tried to refuse the additional beer being poured down my throat, but as hard as I tried, I couldn't speak or scream without choking.

The blonde-haired man took my breasts in his mouth and bit them so hard that I moaned louder with the pain it caused. I could see the enjoyment they all had with each moan, with the next being louder than the last.

Again the blonde-haired man lifted me up almost into a doggy position as the naked man beneath me did things to me that I had never experienced before. As I groaned louder from the pain, the third man turned the stereo up as high as it would go to avoid getting complaints. The man beneath me shouted to his friend to stop until he positioned himself better, and I could feel a bolt of lightning strike throughout my entire body.

Together, they both humped vigorously as the groans turned to screams with agonizing pain, while the other three men watched and waited their turn. One of them pulled my hair back so hard to expose his penis being rubbed across my face and working its way toward my mouth until he found it, with his hands wrapped tightly around my neck, pressing harder and harder into my throat. I couldn't breathe anymore, and once he realized it, he released his pressure. My head was bent back so far, causing excruciating pain until he climaxed, and like the janitor, his junk spewed out of my mouth in every direction. While I was still sandwiched, the other two were still going strong, laughing and telling each other that they could do this all night and that they had lots of time to make that happen.

Tears were running down my face from the unbearable pain. I was still unable to move from whatever drugs they had given me, to the point that I didn't think that I could go on much longer or survive such torture. I just wanted to die to end my suffering. I kept wondering why my sister wasn't there for me when I needed her, and how these men could have so much enjoyment making someone endure as much agony as they were doing to me. I wanted to leave and even go back home to the hell that was much better than this. Why would my sister agree to this kind of torture on me? Then it all started to make sense.

It was then that I heard the blonde man reminding his friends that they had me for the entire night, with my sister's guarantee for their totally satisfaction, and even though I would groan at what they were doing to me, she had assured them that I loved the worst they could possibly do.

In the morning, I woke up fully dressed, lying outside my sister's room. My clothes were drenched with every possible bodily fluid, and I had the worst headache I ever thought possible. When my sister opened her door, she stared at me not only with a look of disgust but maybe also of shock that I actually survived such an ordeal that should have permanently incapacitated me, if not worse. I had no idea where I was, where I had been that night, or whom I was with. It was a classic "Roofies" experience, but the fact that my sister had paid these guys to do what they did to me, showed her true colors as to how evil she really was. Thankfully, they failed with her instructions to overdose me, to death.

Leanne told me how appalled she was at what I had done, and when asked, she denied having any part of such a sadistic event. What I did remember hearing was that my sister was responsible for making this happen, something about a lot of money she paid them, and how much I enjoyed the pain with whatever they could do to me, with the worst pain being the most liked. I also remember them mentioning that I frequented all the dorm parties on campus, challenging the men to try their hardest to hurt me sexually, so as to give me the sexual release I craved.

As I entered her room, Leanne threatened to tell mom and dad what a slut I was but claimed she wouldn't say how she knew. She had me where she wanted me, and I knew it. I begged her not to tell and tried to explain through my foggy mind what had happened that night. All she could say was if she didn't tell, I would owe her big-time. I nodded, asking to take a shower and use her laundry to clean my clothes before going home. I certainly couldn't go home with blood, feces, and urine all over me. As she turned to take me to her shower, I thought I could see a glimpse of her smiling, almost with pride at what she had done, knowing that I had nearly no recollection of what really happened or any of the insidious details.

As she led me to her bathroom, she suddenly pushed past me to get there first, which I thought was a little strange. Then I noticed her hustling to remove a baggie of pills that were on the counter. My mind was racing in wonder if these were the pills that she had given those men to force down my throat while they raped me. I was still at her mercy, not remembering enough about that night with so much booze, until months later when the horrid nightmares of my experience started invading my sleep and the recollection of what really happened started coming back to me in pieces.

When I returned home, my parents asked how

my night with my sister went. All I could say was that it was okay, fearing that she had called them before I got home. When they expressed their approval for me going back again for another visit, my hands started to tremble, and I just said that it wasn't my cup of tea, but I thanked them for the offer, while heading to the bathroom to soak in a hot tub and to inspect my injuries.

I had bruising from head to toe with bite marks starting on my breasts working down to my toes. My backside and privates looked like I had been hit by a bus, and I feared I wouldn't heal. There was bruising on my neck where I had been choked and bruising on my wrists and ankles where I was held down. My only hope was to try to forget what had happened, and it was a lesson learned about how cruel and evil my sister could actually be. How could I ever conceivably think she would change after so many years of being such a horrible beast? It made me wake up to the true reality of life, and not in a good way. She would never change and I would never fall for any of her future attacks again.

CHAPTER 13

School had not been good, and my father's abuse was quickly accelerating again. All I wanted was to be left alone forever in my room. It was several days later when Sharon called asking to meet somewhere. We met at the mall, and when she showed up, she was covered in bruises from her dad's beatings. We sat in the bathroom and cried as we both described our recent experiences. Sharon blurted out that she was going to run away and begged me to go with her. I didn't have to think about it twice and nodded vigorously at the idea. We agreed that we would leave the next morning when our parents went to work. That would at least give us a few hours head start.

In the morning, I headed to Sharon's place with a knapsack and waited outside in the backyard for her to come out, telling her parents we were going to school together to pick out our classes for the following year and that we would be back by dinnertime after studying at the library. Her mom kissed her good-bye, and we headed for the onramp to the 401 highway heading west.

Our destination was Vancouver. We would get jobs and a nice apartment together where no one would harass or abuse us ever again. It sounded great, better than the suicidal thoughts I started having. I never had the nerve to kill myself, remembering the bottle of aspirin my sister gave me when I was six and the multiple pills dumped into me at the university. It was obvious that my bitch sister wanted me dead or to suffer enough that I would do the deed myself. Running away was the next best thing, or so I hoped. My mind remembered what the doctor had told me about either being a victim or a survivor. As I walked silently to the highway thinking about my life, I realized that I had always been a survivor, and I was determined to survive now at any cost, and God help any assholes who thought differently.

Back in those days, it was pretty safe hitch-hiking, and we did it a lot without any problems. One time, I was hitchhiking down a main street in Toronto when a car pulled over, and to my surprise, it was my father driving. I quickly thought of an excuse to give him, but he laughed as I got into the car, assuming that I knew it was him and stuck my thumb out as a funny gesture. We both laughed, agreeing that he was right, but really, it was a very close call.

Sharon and I stood on the onramp of the 401

with both our thumbs stuck out, and the first truck that came along stopped to pick us up. The driver seemed okay when we got into the cab. Sharon sat beside him with me closest to the door. I wasn't going to trust anyone anymore, so a quick exit sounded like a good plan. We headed down the highway toward our destination, but after we traveled a few hours, it started to get dark and all the trouble began.

Sharon had fallen asleep within the first hour, so the driver kept me in conversation, which I wanted no part of. There was something unsettling about him that made me feel uneasy, so I remained polite and appreciative of the ride. I had been through some tough years, so I felt that I was just imagining things. He was grubby and rough looking with so much facial hair covering his entire face, looking almost like a werewolf, but before we got into the truck, Sharon told me that he looked like one of her uncles, and her uncle was a cool guy. She convinced me that we would be fine, so I reluctantly followed her intuition.

I was really tired but fought sleep as best I could with this driver encouraging me to also go to sleep like my friend. I must have dozed off for a few seconds because when I woke up, we were parked along the highway with Sharon still asleep beside him and this guy rubbing his hand up and down her leg toward her privates. The bulge in his pants showed a huge erection, so I elbowed Sharon until she woke up and said that this was our stop. We quickly jumped out of the cab without an explanation. I couldn't help but yell a few obscene words to the guy as he drove off. He left us somewhere on the highway in complete darkness, secluded from everything, except for the frightening animal sounds and trees that surrounded us. We had jumped out so fast that we forgot our knapsacks in the cab with the few things that we had brought with us. We had nothing now but the clothes on our backs and the fourteen dollars in my back pocket. By now, our parents would have noticed that we were gone, and they must have called the school to find out we never showed up to pick our classes, and that the library was closed.

Sharon freaked out a little bit about her bag while I tried to figure out what to do next. The highway was quiet so it had to be sometime after midnight. I wasn't sure what to do until another eighteen-wheeler headed toward us with his high beams on. We couldn't take the risk of a police cruiser finding us, so I immediately stuck my thumb out as he passed by. When I heard the brakes, I turned around to see that he had stopped a few hundred feet down the road flicking his lights to indicate a ride.

Unlike the other trucker, he bombarded us with questions of what we were doing out so late at night in the middle of the highway, as if he actually cared about us. I made up a story that we lost our money, and we were trying to get home to Vancouver and back to our parents. It seemed to satisfy his curiosity, as he pulled back onto the highway. He was a nice man, clean cut, and had pictures of his family taped to his visor. He said that he was only going as far as Saskatchewan but would drop us off where we could crash safely for the night. We thanked him, and again Sharon sat next to him while talking up a storm like she usually did when she wasn't asleep. I closed my eyes to try to get some much-needed sleep, which I lacked from the last ride. This trucker seemed like a very nice man, and I felt safe closing my eyes.

We stopped at a few truck stops, where he bought us some of their lousy sandwiches. It had been such a long time since we ate anything, so it was a real treat for us, and we appreciated it. I made a point of asking him for his mailing address where we could send the money he spent on us. He refused, thanking me for the offer while telling us that he had two daughters our age and he was happy to help us out.

It was very late the next night when I noticed the sign that said, "Welcome to Moose Jaw." If you blinked, you would pass the entire town without noticing it. He turned to us and said that this was as far as he could take us, but he pulled over in front of the Moose Jaw Motel and told us that the owner was his sister, that we should mention his name and she would let us stay there free for the night. We were overjoyed at the offer and thanked him as we got out of the cab, and he drove off.

I remember the clock on the wall in the office as we entered to get a room showing that it was 2:17 a.m. The woman we woke up was very nice and gave us a room close to the office so we could get a good night's sleep, and no one would bother us. In the morning, we woke up at ten, respecting the eleven o'clock check-out time on the door. We quickly took showers and redressed in our filthy clothes.

As we entered the office to check out, she was there waiting for us. I told Sharon to wait outside while I spoke to her, explaining that we had lost our money but that we would work cleaning their rooms until our bill was paid. I also pleaded with her to keep us on for a few more days, working to pay for our keep. She just stared at me, but she was so wonderful and told us that she had gotten a phone call from her brother saying he would pay our bill for the night and not to worry. I thanked her, and as I walked out the door, I took one of their business cards with the intention of sending the money to her once we arrived in Vancouver and got jobs.

We walked through the town in silence as I tried to figure out where exactly Moose Jaw was and how much further it would be to get to Vancouver from here. We noticed that there were so many cops scouring the town and wondered what was going on that caused so much excitement. There was one cop just a few cars ahead of us speaking to a friendly-looking couple. My curiosity got the best of me and I wanted to know what was happening. I told Sharon to wait where she was sitting under a park tree until I came back in a few minutes. Cars were parked along one side of the street where they spoke, so I crawled on my belly along the road to the car that separated us, trying to get close enough to hear what he was saying.

I was in complete shock when I was able to see the wrinkled picture he was holding of Sharon and me. I could hear him say that we were runaways, and there was an "APB" out for us throughout all of Canada until we were found. I was breathless and then shimmied back on my belly to where I had left Sharon, telling her that we had to stay out of sight because the entire country was looking for us.

It was going to be a challenge of my wits to escape detection, but I felt confident that I could get us through this, and I would use every tool I learned to make it happen. It was as if my mind shifted into a higher gear I never knew I had. I was excited, fearless, reckless, and exhilarated all at the same time with the adrenaline pumping inside of me so fast and furiously that I thought my heart would pop out of my chest. I loved it!

When I returned, Sharon was staring off into

another world and freaking out that so many cops were looking for us. She was crying, whining that she missed her mom and even her dad, who she claimed had beaten her so badly. Then she blurted out that the beatings weren't as bad as she made them out to be. I was fixated on her in disbelief, realizing once again that I had been deceived and betrayed with lies by someone I trusted. Then, to my surprise, she confessed that she had exaggerated the truth by actually helping to make the bruises look worse than they really were to get sympathy. I was very upset with her as we headed further into the park, pleading with her to carry out what we started if for no other reason than for my sake, promising her it would be okay once we got to Vancouver.

All she could do was cry hysterically for her mommy, to the point that I had to face the nightmare of going back home with her. Unfortunately, I was running out of pain medication. It was in my knapsack, left on the first truck that picked us up, and I was suffering terribly. My mind raced, thinking I wouldn't be able to make the journey safely by myself without any further altercations traveling alone. I also couldn't exclude the fact that Sharon had such a big mouth, and it was inevitable that everyone would know our plans and the cops would be waiting for me in Vancouver. Of course, she had promised not to tell anyone, but now I knew how weak and deceitful she was, and I didn't have a chance against her big mouth.

We sat in the park for several minutes while she cried until it was causing the kind of commotion I was trying to avoid. Finally, I told her that we would go home and to look around for a pay phone. We were hungry, and with the little money I had left in my pocket, we went to a store close by and bought chocolate bars to keep our energy up. I needed the sugar high to give me the strength to call home, but that would leave us completely broke after paying for the call. I also hoped that if given enough time Sharon might change her mind and we could head back to the highway and continue our journey. No such luck!

Sharon had stopped crying long enough to listen as I dialed my number, telling me that we should call collect. She had done it before several times, and we didn't need to use up the little money we had left, so I was grateful for the suggestion. My mind was still racing, learning that there was always at least one solution to every problem, but she had started crying hysterically again. With the police almost in earshot of us, it was impossible to think clearly, and I had no time to figure something out. I did know that if the police found us, the situation would become a lot worse, so I hung up, pulling our jacket hoods up over our heads, and we took off in the opposite direction of the oncoming cops. We headed for a pay phone that Sharon found as my hands started to tremble. I kept thinking of what I would be returning home to: my sister, my father, school, and the abuse that I didn't think I had enough strength to handle anymore. I would do just about anything to avoid that, but at the same time, I was afraid of just how far I would go to do it.

I stopped several times within the four hundred yards separating us from the next pay phone in a last attempt to change her mind. Sharon was head-strong and totally selfish about going home. Not once did she consider what I would have to go through when I got there.

When I asked why she would come this far before changing her mind, she told me they had had a fight about her behavior, the lack of effort with her school-work and going out to bars. She never mentioned any of the sexual abuse she convinced me was happening that I could relate to. She was actually just looking to get attention and had experienced nothing close to what I went through, and then forced to spend time in a psych ward. I was almost irate with her lies but still had my wits about me. My mind was scrambling desperately to find a way to keep from going home, but with the cops closing in on us, I was out of time and couldn't find an answer.

She begged me to call my parents first, which

took all the strength I had in me to do. I picked up the phone and dialed the operator until I heard the home phone ring. My mother answered crying, and when the operator started to talk, telling her that it was a collect call from Stephanie, I could hear her yell for dad to come to the phone. I made myself perfectly clear that I would hang up if there was any yelling, and I was sure it would happen when my father grabbed the phone from her. Instead, he sounded frightened, saying how glad he was that I had called. He continued to say that they were very sorry again, that things would change, and they wanted us both back as soon as we could get there.

His words meant nothing to me. After all, it was because of him that I was committed to a psych ward. My sister had me raped at the university, and all the kids at school hated me, because of my dad. Why the hell would I want to go back to that? I think I was more afraid of hitch-hiking alone the rest of the way to Vancouver than I was about going back home, but I would if I had to. I was trying very hard to accept their words and maybe take the slim chance that they were both actually being sincere this time. It wasn't an easy choice to make, but I wanted to believe them for once.

When Dad asked where we were and how we got there, I told him that we were in Moose Jaw, Saskatchewan, that the how wasn't important, and I asked if he would promise this time that our home life would be different. He promised profusely, probably with his fingers crossed behind his back, and although he wasn't the trustworthy type, I just wanted it to be true so much that I gave in. Maybe something like this was all he needed to wake up to be a better person, but deep inside, I knew I was kidding myself.

The conversation stalled for a few minutes while he tried to think of how he could get us home. He knew that if the police brought us back, there would be more questions than he wanted or needed, and it could possibly bring out the truth about him, exposing him for the bastard he was. He asked me if there were any trains or buses where we were, but I didn't know so I told him I would find out and call him back.

We found a nice elderly couple on the street and asked where the nearest bus stop or train station was and watched as they pointed to the other side of town. Obviously, the cops hadn't approached them yet, and it was a relief. The problem was that we had to get to the other side of town and past so many more cops to get where we were going. There was only one option, and that was to crawl past the police cruisers and parked cars on our bellies like I had already done successfully. Sharon wasn't up for that, so I threatened her that we had to do it or we could go to jail for running away. I really wasn't sure if my threats were true, but it worked and she agreed, so we headed off toward the station.

One man watching us came up and asked what we were doing under parked cars, so I told him that we were looking for our lost puppy. It was a ruse I was familiar with, and it satisfied his curiosity as he walked away from us, wishing us good luck in finding it.

The oil that the cars left on the asphalt coated our clothes with grease, and we looked like the homeless people we saw when bar hopping in downtown Toronto. That was nothing compared to what we would go through if the cops caught us, so we kept moving until we saw the train station ahead.

As we got closer, we stood up and took our jackets off to enter the station like normal people. The woman behind the counter just kept staring at us as we approached, clearly not knowing what to think about these two children standing before her. I quickly asked where the first train out of Moose Jaw was headed, and she told me there was a train leaving in fifteen minutes to a town several hours north of Toronto, where we could get a transfer, and we could be there by tomorrow night. My eyes lit up because my mother was from that town, and she could arrange a pick-up at the train station for us by my super cool aunt. I visited there once with Mom a few times when we were younger, and it was an amazing trip I would never forget.

I found a pay phone in the station and called my dad back. He answered on the first ring. After the operator did her connection thing, he quickly thanked me for calling back and then asked what was happening. I told him about the train in fifteen minutes, and he told me that he would call the station, pay for the tickets, and then call Rosie to pick us up upon arrival the next night. Sharon was now whimpering beside me so I asked him to please call her parents to tell them that we would be home in a few days, which he promised to do.

I hung up and sat silently in the station until the woman who took tickets called us over and told us that our tickets had been paid for and that we could board the train immediately, departing now in less than four minutes. It was just in the nick of time, as I watched the cops heading toward the station. We would be on the train and gone by the time they got here.

It was a terribly long train ride, and Sharon slept most of the way. I remember wondering how someone could possibly sleep as much as she did when I barely slept at all in days for fear of something happening to us if I did. I stayed awake the entire time, afraid of what was going to happen when I got home. I forced myself to think only of the present, not of the past, and what I would say to Rosie about the circumstances leading us there when we arrived. It would be hours before we arrived, and I had a lot to think about.

We rolled into the station after eight the next night and I was so hungry that my stomach wouldn't stop growling. I couldn't ignore the fact that if she helped slaves, she would help us no matter what the situation was without any explanation or judgment. It had been a few years since I had seen Rosie, but she hadn't changed a bit. She was the woman who rescued the slaves when they fled from a terrible fate of torture and impending death in the 1940's. Although, black slavery ended in the 1860's, there were still pockets in the south where owners still practiced it. In 1942 a Texan family, living on a remote farm, was charged with holding a worker in slavery for four years, repeatedly beating him with whips and chains. Eventually they were caught and sent to prison.

Rosie recognized me immediately at the station as we departed from the train. She was running toward us with open arms. I started to cry just at seeing a happy welcoming face, and ran into her arms. She greeted us with a smile before shaking me lovingly and asking what I was thinking when running away like this. She had heard all of the stories about my dad when he lived there but never thought that his children's lives could be so bad as to do something this reckless. I just held her tightly as she led us to the car and the short ride back to her amazing home. I introduced Sharon as we drove. Everyone felt so comfortable with Rosie because that was the type of person she was; friendly, nonjudgmental, empathetic, and loyal to everyone. She was an icon in the community for all she had done, and everyone loved her.

Sharon tagged along quietly behind us as Rosie and I got reacquainted, still tired from the ride, but she came to life when we entered the house, and it was everything I claimed it to be. There was so much history there, and I was excited to get right into it.

I pulled her over to the old piano she had in the living room and motioned for her to sit down without saying anything, except for the smile on my face that told her it was something I knew she would want to see. Sharon used to play the piano, so she started hitting the keys, which made a terrible sound. She told me that it was so badly out of tune. I laughed as I explained that it wasn't just an ordinary piano. In fact, it provided a valuable asset to Rosie's work and had been specifically modified, undetectable to the naked eye, and would be a huge part of her legacy saving so many lives.

She looked at me like I was crazy until I told her to stop and wait while I pressed certain selected keys in rapid succession. After the last key, there was a loud grinding noise that she didn't understand, and she looked questioningly at me. The entire room was paneled for a reason, and as the noise stopped, I pointed to the part of the wall behind us that opened unexpectedly, exposing a very narrow stairway leading up to the second floor.

I remember the look on her face when it happened, and I could tell it frightened her. She had never seen anything like it before. She asked what the hell was happening as I took her hand and led her toward the opening. I could feel her hands tremble from the unknown. She was probably wondering what I had gotten her into, but I reassured her that it was okay and there was nothing to fear.

As we climbed to the top of the staircase, there were several small bedrooms built deliberately to avoid detection from both the outside and inside of the house. There were several sets of bunk beds in each room. Sharon was still totally confused as I started to tell her about the slaves who were hidden by Rosie when they escaped years ago. At the far end of the room, also hidden by a paneled wall, was another set of stairs that led down to a tunnel she had built beneath the house. This was an escape route to protect anyone needing safe passage, and that led far out beyond the fields at the back of her home.

The tunnel extended five hundred yards to the

east, but after so many decades, it became overgrown with weeds and roots from the trees in the surrounding woods. Everything started to make sense to her now, and she smiled for once at what a neat house I had brought her to and the history behind it.

My father was well known in the town for being the worst kind of racist, and everyone hated him for it. Many kids at my school were black and brown and were wonderful kids from great families. They never judged me and accepted me for who I was, but they stayed clear of my father because of his bigoted attitude. It was absolutely forbidden for me to have those kinds of kids as friends, and he constantly warned me that I would be severely punished if I ever brought any of them to the house. This was old-school parenting, but I learned to overcome it with the lies and deception that had become a part of my life, and I got to be very good at it.

After the tour upstairs, we went back down to where Rosie was waiting for us with a smile. Sharon would repeatedly tell me what an amazing aunt I had. She was surprised to hear that she wasn't really a blood-related aunt, but just a long-time friend of my mothers, and out of respect we were supposed to call her auntie. She was terrific and never pressured us into telling her why we ran away. For some weird reason, I always thought that she knew the kind of father my mother married, but we both just kept quiet and enjoyed the visit with each other. Finally, after a delicious home-cooked meal, she stood up and said that we had to call our parents. Sharon jumped at the opportunity while I was hesitant and stood back, squirming at the thought. I remember Rosie saying that no matter what happened at home, it was a lot less dangerous than hitch-hiking, and that we were very fortunate that nothing bad had happened to us. Sharon and I just shared a quick glance at each other without mentioning the creepy trucker who first picked us up.

I stayed silent, saying nothing of what my father and sister had done to me for my mother's sake. Rosie loved my mother, she had known her since kindergarten, and in a small town there weren't very many secrets. Rosie had also known my father from way back, but since he never came to visit with us, I was convinced that there was a story behind why, and decided not to ask and open up that can of worms. I wasn't prepared for the answer, and I doubted she would have told me either being my mom's daughter.

Sharon was excited, speaking with her mom as the tears rolled down her cheeks, apologizing for what she had done. When Rosie turned to me, gesturing that I was next to use the phone, I reluctantly made the call out of respect for her, and she noticed the hesitation. I wanted to stay and live there with her, but when I asked, she told me that she was a loner and didn't have the patience to deal with children of any age, and that was the reason she never had kids.

CHAPTER 14

It was arranged that we would stay at Rosie's overnight and then catch the next train to Toronto in the morning. My father would pick us up at the station there that night. Sharon was so excited and kept me awake the entire night talking about how great it was going home and continued saying how lucky I was to have such a great aunt living in such an amazing house. In contrast, I worried how bad the beatings would be after my dad dropped Sharon off, and we got back to that demonic house where the black cloud hovered overhead.

Nothing had changed on the street, including the black cloud, as we pulled into the driveway, with the sun shining everywhere else on the street but our house. It was then that I truly knew what that cloud meant; it signified no hope for those who lived there. I hesitated at the front door, but my father grabbed my hand and forced me inside.

My mother flew toward me, crying her eyes out

and hugging me so tight it almost hurt. She ushered me into that horrible kitchen I hated so much with all those terrible memories I desperately tried to forget, especially the conversation where my sister had them agree to adopt me out to another family.

I sat down to the spaghetti dinner she had made for me, but just looking at it made me sick, remembering when it was thrown onto the floor while Dad assaulted me until I vomited. Too many memories flooded back into my head as the nausea started to rise. My father ordered my mother out of the room within minutes of my arrival, and as she left, my father looked at me with those dark, deadened eyes, pounding his fist onto the table, and demanding to know my intentions about returning to school.

I glared back at him with just as much force, now staring eye to eye with every ounce of strength I had. I yelled back at him in a voice I never knew I had, but one that he would understand. It was the kind of voice that usually came from him to someone else, and not to him from anyone who dared to try. I growled at him this time, telling him, "Screw school, and screw you, you bastard!"

I didn't see it coming until the blow to my head hit me so hard that it knocked me off the chair onto the floor, and I briefly blacked out. As I slowly came to, I could hear my mother yelling at him to stop. Blood trickled from my head as I tried to lift myself from the kitchen tiles, noticing that one of the tiles had cracked during the impact. I actually had a piece of the tile sticking out of my head. Mom was hysterical, but it was such a normal occurrence that I hardly noticed. Staggering upward, I took the napkin she had placed by my plate, grabbed the chair and lifted it back to its upright position. It took a couple of minutes for me to focus on where I was and what had just happened, and when I tried to speak, the taste of iron from my blood trickled into my mouth. My mother stood at the doorway, trying hard to make her way toward me and tend to my wound, but she was physically pushed away by my father, who forced her out of the room again.

The fight was on, and now I had to see it through. I had learned a lot from my trip with Sharon and what was necessary of me to do if I was to survive this wretched life. I had to fight back, and I was not going to let him win again this time. I didn't care anymore, and I had had enough!

I wasn't sure to what degree I had to fight, but I wasn't going to be a punching bag anymore. As he grabbed me around the throat, I could hear my mother scream at him like she had done the many times before from the top of the stairs. He was going to kill me if he didn't stop, and I could tell by the look in his eyes that I had no time to stop and think about my next move. I just grabbed and squeezed his crotch with every ounce of strength left in my hand and then ran past him, quickly turning cautiously for fear of his retaliation. He slumped to the floor in pain, grabbing himself where it counted, and I knew then that it wouldn't be long before he'd come after me. I ran past Mom upstairs to my room, searching for any kind of weapon I could use to protect myself. I was terrified, heading for the window to see if it could be used as a quick exit, but without any luck. I backed myself up against the bedroom door to hear what was being said in an effort to give me insight as to how I could escape or keep from being killed.

My heart was pounding faster than it ever had before, while the adrenaline and extreme stress were running ramped through my brain. My mind was exploding with strategies and thoughts to finally become a tool I could use. I was proud of myself for finally taking a stand against my father.

I was learning that you had to be one step ahead of everyone else in life who was trying to screw you in one way or another, and my father and sister were at the top of the list. If there was nothing else I learned from life at home, it was that no child should ever have to endure this much suffering. I was so jealous of the other kids at school, listening to them in the halls bragging about how great their parents were; their family vacations, and the love in their voices as they spoke. I wanted what they had so badly, but with my life, there weren't many choices, and if I was going to survive, then I needed to fight or die trying.

Failing to find a way out of my room, I knew my only recourse was to prepare myself in case he would come at me again, and I was worried at the outcome. I had to do something, but I wasn't sure what. I had taken as much abuse that I possibly could and was pacing back and forth in my tiny bedroom, frantically trying to figure out what to do next. I had street smarts, just not book smarts most people spent years at university to achieve, and I didn't want that with what those bastards had done to me. I had to remind myself again that I would not be a victim any longer, but there was this penetrating rage inside of me that made me too terrified for my own comfort. I had to somehow find a way to harness it.

While my parents were verbally fighting in the kitchen, I went into their bedroom to call Sharon. I cut her short with her babbling on about how great it was to be back home again, blah, blah, blah. "Bullshit!" I told her how bad it was for me and that I could not live here another minute with my father trying to kill me, but I had nowhere to go and asked her if she knew anyone who could help me.

She thought for a minute before naming her friend Dave, who might help me out and maybe let me stay with him until I could get settled with a job and a place to live. She gave me his address and phone number and then asked me to give her a half hour to get in touch with him first to let him know I needed help and that I was coming. All I could think was that I didn't have a half hour to wait, and by that time, it could be too late. I barricaded my bedroom door with my dresser and took the screen off the tiny window I could barely squeeze through while starting to pack another bag.

CHAPTER 15

The waiting was killing me, and I was ready to run before the bastard came upstairs. In desperation, I pulled the window out and jumped down two stories, heading to Sharon's place instead of waiting. I stood at her bedroom window, throwing stones until she opened it. She had reached Dave, and it was arranged that I would meet him downtown close to his house at midnight.

I knew the buses were still running at night after eleven, where a bus would take me to the subway, dropping me off right where I was meeting him. I barely had enough money left from our trip, and I was thankful that it was just enough for a bus ticket and transfer. I had a small bag packed with only the necessities I needed, and didn't care about the rest.

I met Dave at a coffee shop, and with Sharon's description, I had no problem identifying him when I arrived. Dave was a definite party guy and stood out from the rest of the men in the coffee shop when

I spotted him. He was very weathered from the sun, the life he led, or the drugs he did, but I was too inexperienced to tell. I was desperate and wasn't going to look a gift horse in the mouth. He was very different from the guys I knew at school and had an intriguing quality about him that was hard to describe. This was my only option and opportunity, and this guy was going to be the one to give it to me. Over the years, I had become dead inside, but I would make nice with him until he agreed to help me anyway he could. What I didn't realize was that he wanted the whole enchilada the first night. I didn't care, and it wasn't as if I was new to sex, so I would give him whatever he wanted. I casually started seducing him with hugs and kisses while rubbing his inner thigh until I could feel his crotch reacting to my touch. I was grateful, and decided I would do almost anything to finally escape my father's clutches.

Dave was a very attractive man as far as I was concerned. He lived in a well-known rooming house right in the center of downtown Toronto, known for drugs, loose women, and questionable principles. He wasn't aware of my age, and for me, it didn't matter, but with him being almost twice my age and for both our sakes, I lied about my age so I wouldn't be referred to as "jail-bait" and scare him away.

It was a unisex rooming house with three women and four men living in separate rooms with a common kitchen and bathroom, and poor quality decor that I wasn't used to. The common areas were filthy and neglected, and the smell was appalling.

It was late when we left the coffee shop and arrived at the house, so I didn't have a chance to meet the others. He led me to his room on the first floor, which basically was just a bedroom with little furniture and very poor décor. I thought it to be rather dowdy. It was very suitable for a single party man who would rather spend all his money on drugs, booze, and wild women. I never considered myself loose, but escaping such a catastrophic lifestyle at home, I felt like this was a positive step forward. This would be my life now, so I despairingly accepted it and would do my best to maintain what I could of myself and move forward no matter where life took me.

I was exhausted from the trip across Canada, not to mention Sharon, who exhausted me with her crying, sniveling, and talking my ear off the entire time. I gave as little information about myself to Dave as possible, keeping him on a need-to-know-basis. There was only one bed in his room, so he told me that I could have the left side and he would take the right. I agreed as I fell exhausted onto the bed with no problem. He offered me one of his shirts as pajamas, which I forgot to pack, and I fell back down onto the bed instantly into a deep and peaceful sleep that I hadn't had in years. Although my future was unclear,

I actually felt safe with this man. I couldn't fathom any reasonable explanation for it, but with him just being here for me now was the difference between life and death, and I appreciated it.

When I woke up in the morning, I could tell it was early, noticing the darkness through the window. Dave's alarm had gone off, but before getting out of bed, he took me in his arms and told me how beautiful I was and that my body was like that of a princess everyone would want to take advantage of. Of course, I fell for that line once again because it was what I needed to hear, and as he undressed me, he climbed on top of me. I could feel something that I had rarely felt before. It was total passion with the softest loving strokes that were so different from the rapes and sex that were always forced upon me. It was so sensuous, perfect, and it made me feel like the princess he claimed me to be. For the second time I felt that I was falling in love again, like I had done with Johnny, only this time, I was desperately praying it would be genuine. That was something I never knew anything about, and desperately wanted more than anything. He was soft yet muscular, and his chest hairs beneath my face felt great as our bodies combined into one. I was consumed in the moment, and it felt so good wrapped safely in his arms. Within minutes, I was convinced that this was pure love, at least until I got to know him better in the coming days with the truth, and a different direction I hadn't planned on.

I would find out later that Dave was nothing but a womanizer and very good at it, but now that we had met, I knew he would change for his true love, me. He could make any woman he chose melt into his arms instantly while they slept together. His kiss was soft and passionate, yet probing into my mouth, making me feel as though he too had found his special soul mate for life. I was stupid, naïve, and too young to tell the difference, with no real relationship experience in my life at my age to compare him against, but I knew what I liked, what I needed, what I wanted, and I prayed that this was it.

It was a Friday with the weekend approaching, and after we made love, he dressed for work with a passionate good-bye kiss, telling me that I would soon meet everyone in the house when he came home from work that evening at six o'clock. It frightened me a little, not knowing what to expect, but it was something that I had to do, and I felt very safe with him by my side, so I tried to look excited at the thought of meeting everyone. He kissed me good-bye one more time, leaving me to think about him the entire day, waiting anxiously for him to return.

I knew nothing about Dave except that he rescued me from the clutches of my sick, demonic family. When I was younger, I used to dream of a prince like him carrying me away to a far-off land, far enough away to finally find the happiness I deserved, so this was just a glorious start to my fantasy. He would be my man for life, we would get married, have beautiful children, and I would feel safe and secure forever. It was more of a fairytale than a fantasy, and it nearly broke my heart when I soon found out the truth.

Unfortunately, I found that Dave was not that kind of prince, just a "free spirit" clear to the bone. He didn't do commitments or anything else for that matter that might tie him down to just one woman. He also didn't come home that night when he said he would and left me to fend for myself when meeting the others in the house. I wasn't sure what he told them about me, but he must have said something because they all knew my name and why I was there.

My first visitor was Cathy with a "C," who lived in the room directly next to Dave. She seemed nice, but there was something about her that rubbed me the wrong way. The truth would soon unfold, shattering my love for Dave and destroying our fairytale future together.

Next, I met Ingrid. I was warned that she was extremely weird and a recluse who lived across the hall. She had a room full of cats and was so unsociable that when I knocked on her door, she hesitated to answer, probably because she didn't recognize me through the peep-hole in her door. She eventually invited me in, insisting that I sit on her special chair that stuck out from the rest of her furniture in the middle of her room. I found out later that she was terrorized by everyone in the house because of her strange habits, and I felt sorry for her because she reminded me of myself. The chair she insisted other tenants to sit on was very special to her in that she had her cats pee on it regularly, and it gave her so much satisfaction getting back at everyone for their taunting and terrorizing.

Mike upstairs was really nice, but he had several small bruises on the inside of his arms, indicating what seemed to be needle marks. I also noticed several empty bottles of alcohol scattering his room when I entered. I found out later that he was a heroin addict and an alcoholic, but he was very well liked by everyone because he kept to himself and minded his own business. I wasn't sure what heroin was, but I knew that I hated needles, so I kept away from him as much as possible. He was very friendly, saying that we would be friends while I lived there, and then he asked where Dave was. Like the others, he knew I was staying with Dave. Everyone in the house knew where he was, but they thought it best if I found out for myself, so he changed the subject. He had a secretive look about him when he spoke, but I had no answer for him and started questioning him as the friend he said we would be. Mike just shrugged and told me that it would all come together for me soon. After all, Dave did say that he would be home at six that night and now it was after midnight.

I was getting tired and headed back to our room. Dave had sliding doors between his and Cathy's room that weren't able to close completely. There was a huge bureau that blocked the sliding doors to their connecting rooms, something like that of a formal dining room that connected to the living room in a regular home.

After I left Mike, he mysteriously appeared at our open door and pointed out the slight opening. He sat down on the bed and asked if I had noticed it yet. I told him that I had just realized it before he came but wasn't sure what he was getting at. He put his finger to his lips, indicating for me to stay very silent, and it would soon become obvious. The mischievous look on his face and tone in his voice frightened me a little with what he was getting at as he put a glass of Johnny Walker in my hand, saying it would help soften the blow with what was about to happen. I hated games, but he had a point to make so I waited patiently for whatever it was, hoping it wouldn't hurt.

Still confused, I sat there with him, listening to nothing except the stereo playing softly until I broke the silence, telling him what a wonderful man Dave was and how we were soul mates with the perfect kind of love we would share forever.

Mike got up to turn the stereo off for the full effect of what would happen next. I started to object, but no sooner had I finished my sentence than I could hear two people groaning in what could only be a sexual encounter in her room. He reached out, stood me up, and pulled me closer to the door with his finger pressed to his lips, determined to keep me very quiet. I wasn't interested in Cathy's love life, but it seemed really important for Mike to have me listen. He lifted me up over the bureau to expose Cathy in bed with a man, having what seemed like incredible sex. I was embarrassed and asked to be let down, but Mike insisted that I continue watching for a few more minutes.

I was getting very uncomfortable until the man in Cathy's bed sat up, reaching for a bottle of water on her bedside table, revealing that the man in bed with her was Dave. I wanted to scream, but Mike had covered my mouth as if expecting it. He let me down gently onto the floor and seemed content exposing the truth about the man I couldn't stop talking about. Mike just kept telling me that this was reality and that Cathy and Dave had been an item for the many years he had known them. He went on to say that Cathy grew used to his indiscretions and had accepted him for who he was, hoping that one day he would settle down and she would be there waiting for him.

I was in shock and wasn't sure what to do next.

I told Mike as calmly as I could that I was going to bed, hiding my emotions and tears until he left the room. I fell onto the bed, burying my head into my pillow so as not to be heard while I cried for hours until I fell asleep. I would figure out what to do in the morning, but I was so devastated that my dream of finding love had once again been shattered into pieces. I had nowhere else to go except home, and that would never be an option again. I would rather die, but I fought those thoughts that were constantly crossing my mind. I needed to toughen up to life, as Mike so boldly tried to teach me. I just didn't know how to do it.

When I finally dragged myself out of bed in the morning, I decided that I would get a job and maybe find a room in another one of the landlord's rooming houses. I went to the kitchen to find something quick to eat when I ran into another Kathy, with a "K." She was really nice and had spent the night there with her boyfriend, Roger. We were having a good conversation when Roger came into the kitchen after his shower with only a towel around his waist, which embarrassed me. I wasn't use to this kind of communal living. Kathy asked me who I was there with, and when I told her Dave, she just smirked, knowing what a womanizer he was from experience and wondering what a young kid like me was doing with a guy like him. It was obvious that

I was underage and definitely looking for love in all the wrong places when I chose Dave to be with. She hit me with so many questions that I wasn't prepared to answer. I just stayed silent, while she looked at me empathetically as if she understood what was happening. She had run into Dave and Cathy earlier in the night at one of the local bars. They had come home together, and then he quietly slithered into Cathy's room to avoid me. It was all making sense to her now after meeting me and the reason why he was so careful sneaking into her room.

Dave came home from work the following evening at six o'clock and he no sooner came into the room than I asked him why he hadn't come home the night before, as promised. I tried hard to be as cool as I could while being very hurt, and insisting that he tell me who he was with. He just smiled an irritating smile that upset me, remembering the incredible passion we had shared together our first night, as if it was nothing now, with all the wonderful things he had said to me that made me feel so loved.

He got angry, telling me that I just couldn't walk into his life and expect him to drop everything since he was helping me out. I told him that he was right and asked if I could leave my bag there for a few days until I returned for it later once I found other accommodations. He nodded his approval in such an easy manner for him, as I walked out the door in search of what was known as a "shelter for women."

I walked along Queen Street, not far from where Dave lived, for what seemed like hours, asking everyone I met if they knew of a shelter that I could go to. There were no definitive answers, so I just kept walking. Finally, I sat down on the stoop of a store, wondering how a thirteen-year-old kid was going to make it all alone in downtown Toronto.

I was hungry and had no money. A street bum came up to me around midnight and told me that I was on his stoop and he would kill me if I didn't move, so I quickly got up and started walking again. Queen Street became a very scary place late at night with all the homeless people coming out of the woodwork, and I was actually worried that something would happen to me and how my mother would react to the cops telling her I was dead. I was lucky to find another stoop close by down the street and curled up in the corner by the door away from the freezing winds that were thrashing through the streets.

It was a chilly November night, and I wasn't sure what to do next. I must have fallen asleep because when I woke up, the sun was out and people were bustling to get to work. When I looked down at my feet, I found some loose change someone had thrown at me, thinking I was just another homeless bum, and with all things considered, I guess I was. I was embarrassed because I wasn't the kind of person who would beg for money, but I appreciated it just the same. There was a grocery store that I passed on the way to my stoop, so I put the money in my pocket and started walking back to the store.

As I entered, I counted the money to find it was $1.50. I knew I couldn't buy much with that, and then I noticed a shelf of breads and cakes at a discounted price in front by the cash register. They had a pound cake for only fifty-seven cents, and a little further on, there was a cup filled with plastic forks and knives. I picked up the pound cake and a knife, paid for it at the counter, and left the store, hoping that my stoop hadn't been taken while I was gone. I was relieved when I returned and it was still empty. I looked at the cake so hungrily that I could have eaten the entire thing right then and there. I took the knife out of the wrapper and started to cut the cake into seven equal pieces, thinking that I could eat one piece each day, allowing me to eat for an entire week. It wasn't much, but it was all I had to work with until I decided my next move. I was excited that I had something to eat every day, but with the kinds of people who surrounded me, I knew that I would have to hide it or maybe die protecting it. I was so scared, thinking now that I should have stayed with Dave. At least it was a safe place and off the streets away from so many weird and dangerous people.

While I was sitting there dividing my loaf, the store owner showed up, irritated at my presence, and shooed me away before the store was about to open. Now it made sense to me why the homeless people only came out at night when the stores were closed. I had to find somewhere else to go for the day, and as I got up to leave, a passerby told me of a shelter where I could get some fresh clothes, a hot meal, and a warm bed for the night.

As she turned away, she threw a two-dollar bill toward me, which I picked up and tried to return to her, thinking that she had dropped it accidently. I wasn't good at this homeless stuff, and she looked shocked as I handed it back to her. She did accept it with a confused facial expression and continued on her way. I turned to make my way toward the shelter she mentioned, but I stood in front of the door, hesitating to go inside.

While I was standing there, one of the counselors excused herself as she reached past me for the door handle, and then she turned back toward me, motioning for me to come inside with her. My whole life had been dependent on doing what I was told to do, so I followed her in while scanning the room, which was full of the worst kinds of street people I never thought I would meet in my life.

I accepted her help as she led me to the front desk. She told me to first register and then come to her office where we could talk in private. It was a quiet conversation, so I didn't give away who I was, and she could feel my tension and apprehension while she did most of the talking. When she asked if I needed some clothes, I just nodded. She stood up and led me to their closet filled with women's clothes. When I told her that I didn't have any money, she assured me that everything in their building was free. I browsed through each item until I found something that would fit and proceeded to the bathroom. When she left me alone to change, I found that the clothes fit perfectly. I quickly walked out of the change room to find her waiting for me outside the door. I didn't see any bedrooms or a kitchen with the hot food I was told about, but I felt so much better wearing fresh clothes, and that was good enough for me, because I still had my loaf cake.

I was embarrassed to stay at the shelter but more so scared because of the types of people who would be squeezed in tightly, sleeping next to me on another small cot. I spent the day there and left returning to my stoop after eating the meals they had served throughout the day. I slept on the street for days until it got so cold outside that I couldn't stand it anymore. I started walking back to Dave's place, where I was greeted by everyone in the house, except for Dave, because of course he and Cathy weren't home.

Kathy with a "K" offered to let me stay with her

for the night, and I graciously accepted. She was great toward me but she had just broken up with her boyfriend, Roger, so I guessed that she needed someone to cry to. After hours of talking about her broken relationship, she asked me what my plans were. I didn't know what to tell her because I didn't have any plans.

She was very helpful in constructing a plan for me to get a job. They were hiring across the street from the rooming house at Bittner's Meat and Delicatessen, and she was sure that if I played my cards right, I could get the job at the lunch counter. I would do that in the morning after a hot shower, and I hoped I had the confidence in myself to get the job I knew I could do.

Just as she said, I went to the store, applied for the job and got it. Kathy would let me stay with her until I started getting paid, and I was very grateful to her for helping me out. It was then that I knew we would be good friends for a long time.

CHAPTER 16

By the end of December, I had enough money to get my own room in the same rooming house, though I was reluctant to rent even if there happened to be one available. When I popped by that morning to visit Mike, I found him looking very gray in the face, and then seconds later, he died right in my arms from an overdose of heroin and frothing at the mouth. It was something I wasn't prepared for, and it totally freaked me out, but I showed no expression as I looked around at the others who made it seem like this was a just a natural way of life there in the city. Fortunately for me, though under such terrible circumstances, Mike's room became available.

I took his room with his furniture included, and the landlord was happy he didn't have to remove it. I just felt safe being surrounded by Mike's personal items and his spiritual presence, feeling secure with all he had taught me since we met. He was like my guardian angel who protected me against my worst fears, and I loved him for it.

The police and ambulance came quickly. I made myself scarce so as not to get involved in case there was another APB out for me. I knew right then that I would never touch that kind of a drug. I was so naïve not to see that everyone else in the house was doing some kind of drug. I knew nothing about street drugs and when they asked me to join them I told them that I had no money to contribute, thinking that would be enough to stop them from asking me again.

Unfortunately for me, they all pooled their money together to give me a freebee, which I felt I had to do to be accepted and stay friends with them all. I really needed people in my life after sleeping on the street for so long. I had always been a loner for as long as I could remember, so it felt really good to be accepted, and this was my life now, whether I liked it or not. I couldn't think of anywhere else I would rather be in a world I knew nothing about, and I felt I could learn a lot living with these people in the house.

After snorting the drug they called cocaine, I was feeling like I was at the top of the world and could accomplish anything in life. I got invited by everyone to go out to the local bar called the Selby Hotel. It was just around the corner, and draft beer was twenty cents a glass. In an attempt to fit in, I joined them even though I didn't like the taste, and although I wasn't of age to drink, I was with Selby regulars, so the bartender never asked for any ID. I must have consumed more than five glasses of beer that were set in front of me as I tried to keep up with everyone else. I was getting wobbly while the beer went through me like a facet, staggering to the bathroom. I had a job to go to the next day, so I excused myself and stumbled home.

In the morning, my headache was so bad that I just wanted to stay in bed all day with an ice pack and bottle of aspirin, but that wasn't going to happen. The migraines caused by my spine were so bad at times that I soon realized the booze was adding to the pain.

Afraid I would lose my job, I slid out of bed, showered, and made my way across the street to start work. The boss was very impressed with me from the start, but I became nervous when he asked me for my birth certificate and Social Insurance Number. I calmly told him that I would present it once the lawyer finished probating my parent's will after their recent deaths, something Mike had told me to say if I was asked, just to buy time. He was right on with the advice, and it was well received with sorrow for my loss. He told me to give it to him when I could.

I worked hard at my job and he surprised me a week later by giving me the snack bar to run on my own, with no supervision. A raise came with the promotion, and I became great at it, supervising two employees under me. My life was looking as good as it could get, except for the hangovers I got drinking with my new friends almost every night at the Selby.

After my day was over and I started walking home, tears clouded my eyes as I wished that I could tell Mike how much I appreciated him teaching me the things in life I didn't know. Somehow, while lying on his bed where he died, I felt that he was looking down on me and was still there when I needed him, something like what Bernie had done for me growing up. A grave sense of loss came over me as I remembered all the things Mike had taught me. All I could do now was look up toward the ceiling with the hope he could somehow hear me thank him. I knew from the start that Mike was a manipulator, only because he told me that everything he got in life was because of it. There was a lesson in what he was telling me; I wasn't sure what it was, but it seemed to work well for me when I tried.

Mike was dead, and I certainly didn't want to be like him ever with the drugs or alcohol addiction or to end up dead and alone after an overdose in some stranger's arms, but I appreciated the care he showed toward me, helping me to fight this world one day at a time, and I loved him for it. He had toughened me up too, so much that I somehow felt I could actually survive this ominous world that had hurt me so badly, and could no longer consume me moving forward.

School had always been on my mind, but there was a teacher strike heading into its second month, so there was no chance of me going back. I was really happy at Bittner's, and I had friends for the first time in my life. I was making money and happy living in Mike's room.

My room was about three hundred square feet with a sunroom that backed onto a park forest with gorgeous trees that I really enjoyed. That together with a bottle of wine and some rock music playing really loud made me finally happy and away from my childhood memories. My door was always open when I was home, and I always welcomed everyone when they visited. No one ever bothered me, and I felt safe. These were my friends now, and I loved them regardless of who they were or what they did.

CHAPTER 17

Then from out of nowhere one evening, a new woman moved into the house. Her name was Misty, which alone should have sent up a red flag, but I learned never to judge people after Mike died. She was really nice, but when she came into my room, it was very late at night, and I had to go to work first thing in the morning. I desperately needed sleep, living this kind of lifestyle, and I didn't want to compromise my job for anything. When I politely asked her to leave, she reluctantly left, and I assumed that she went back to her own room downstairs.

With all that was happening to me so fast I found it hard to sleep at night, always worrying if the police would come and take me back home. I got into the habit of smoking a joint at night to help me sleep, and I hadn't been asleep long before I woke up to someone lying beside me with his or her arm across my chest. I had no idea who the hell was in my bed.

As I turned over, I saw her blond hair and felt

her perfectly manicured hands caressing my breasts. I was totally exhausted and a little stoned from the joint, so it took me awhile to understand what was going on. She proceeded to tell me that she was there to help me, that she was onto me with my age, and if I was going to survive in the downtown world, then I needed to learn as much as I could from the one she considered to be the best at it, herself.

I still didn't understand what she was getting at, so I just lay there, wondering what she was trying to tell me. As I pushed her hand off my breasts, she poured some powder into my nose, telling me that as women, we needed to know how to be satisfied. I was angrier than anything with the intrusion, but the drug she forced on me and with me having to get up for work in only a few short hours, really pissed me off. I had no time for any bullshit, especially from her. She proceeded to go down between my legs for the full Misty experience until I threw her off of me and ordered her leave. She was upset with my rudeness, and that may have been the reason she returned shortly later. I was mortified by her advances toward me, mostly because I wasn't that type of person, but the MDA she poured into my nose had seduced me to the point that I had little control over myself, and things were just happening too fast. I learned later that MDA was a love drug that couples took to enhance their sexual pleasures, and that might have been okay if I had been with a man, but I still hated street drugs except for the little coke and pot I willingly took, and if I was to take another drug, I wanted it to be of my own free will.

In the morning, I woke up alone and made my way to the room Misty claimed to rent. I pounded on the door until some guy by the name of Steve answered. I pushed past him, barging through the door, demanding to see Misty. He was shocked at my demands and told me that he was the tenant and Misty was a hooker he had hired the night before, but she had already left. I apologized for the disturbance, explaining with limited information how she had barged into my room, hoping that he would relay the message to her should she come by again. I was not pleased with her behavior and would take further measures if she tried to contact me again. There may have been a threat or two I made, stating that if he could not control his whores I would have him evicted from the house. I may have overstepped my bounds, but Steve could tell by the anger in my eyes that I wasn't one to be screwed with, so he apologized, promising to speak to her if he ever saw her again.

After that night, all I could think about was Misty, pushing the MDA on me and the sexual encounter that I had always been taught was not right for any woman to do to another woman. I just wanted to make sure that she stayed as far away from me as possible. The worst part were her threats that if I didn't comply with her advances, she would tell everyone my age, call the police, and have me sent home to my parents. I was almost sixteen and frightened of what she could do to me. I would die first before going back home, and the only reason I had inhaled her drug was the belief that if I let her do what she wanted, it would quickly be over and she would leave forever.

Misty was a stripper in one of the local strip clubs downtown, or so I learned the next day, but while I was lying next to her in bed, she expected me to do the same to her as she did to me, and I refused. She got so mad at me, but I started screaming until other tenants came to find out what was happening. She ran for the door before anyone saw her, and the next day, I spoke to Paul, the landlord, who eighty-sixed her out of the rooming house permanently.

I was so upset over what had happened that I fought to go to work the next day, worrying if she was going to show up at my job or call the police on me. After a few days, I found out that there were warrants out on her for serious crimes she had committed, and it was then that I realized she wouldn't get the police involved. She only used that ruse to create a panic with me to get what she wanted, and it worked, with another lesson learned.

Living downtown was something that I never

thought would cause so much stress being a young woman on my own, but Misty warned me that it would only get worse if I didn't toughen up. It seemed to be a commonality that everyone was trying to teach me, and I gave it a lot of thought in the coming days.

Then, I experienced downtown Yonge Street during Halloween. It was as much a spectacle as it was dangerous with the "gay walk" starting at Bloor Street and heading south. It was a time when gays were coming out of the closet, but no one was quite sure of the public's reaction. The "straights" were disgusted and constantly harassing them, when all the gays wanted was to be themselves, together in public, and treated no differently than any other normal couple. It was the seventies with underground gay bars popping up all over Toronto. People were not very receptive, and the reason "gay bashings" grew throughout the city.

It was also the same time when the newspaper published the vicious death of nine-year-old shoeshine boy Emanuel Jacques; brutally murdered on the roof of a downtown apartment building by a sadistic monster in the neighborhood. It was a violent crime with the entire city in an uproar. Now, after forty plus years, it is still an appalling memory, with that monster becoming eligible for parole in 2019.

The crimes were cruel, senseless, and it just proved

how animalistic people were becoming with their appetite to disregard human life, their need to feel superior over those they could desecrate and scar for life; both physically and emotionally. These animals would prey on the young, the weak, the aged, and the most vulnerable, regardless of their gender. In my opinion, there was no prison sentence long enough that could possibly begin to repair the damages that these monsters caused their victims. Every day I showered, I couldn't help but see the many cigarette burn scars on my body, the scars from the beatings I survived, or the years it took for my fingernails to grow back after being sadistically torn off with pliers during an attack, just to inflict pain on me, and to hear me beg for my life. Then, of course, now after decades, there are still the nightmare flashbacks from the rapes and molestations that have left the unseen scars; those hard to hide and may never completely heal.

In this unkind world where I needed to survive, I decided to attend a self-defense class for women. It was a free class and lasted only a couple of hours, but it taught me how to avoid trouble, how to be aware of my surroundings, and how to drop an attacker, no matter what his size, to his knees, in seconds. My favorite defense tactic was going for the throat and then the groin, and being an attractive young woman living in downtown Toronto, I knew I would use it more than I wanted to, and did, leaving one bastard groaning in the same alley he dragged me into.

Finally, I was getting fed up with the downtown life, the constant drinking, occasional drugging, and the rooming house drama where I lived. The teachers' strike was finally coming to an end, and it was now or never if I wanted to get an education.

CHAPTER 18

It was time to go back to school and finish my education. I couldn't go back to the previous school where the kids teased, taunted, and scared me, so I decided to register at a school that was much better, and where they held you to a higher standard, and no one would know me. I knew that I was smarter than anyone thought, so I chose Sir John A. McDonald in the east end of Toronto. It was a high-caliber school, and I knew I could do it if I worked hard enough for it.

I still worked at Bittner's, but the owner let me change my shift to evenings, and I appreciated that. It wasn't easy getting up at 4:00 a.m. to shower, catch two subways and then a forty-minute bus ride to get there, returning back downtown by 5:00 p.m. to go to work until 9:30 p.m., but I was determined to do it. It didn't leave me much time for the three to four hours of studying and homework I needed to do for the next day, and many times, I didn't get to sleep until 3:00 a.m.

I forgot how much homework there was in school. I often depended on the guys in the rooming house to wake me after they had been partying until 4:00 a.m., and many days, I woke up to them shoving me into the shower with the freezing cold water running down my body to wake me up. They claimed that I wouldn't wake up otherwise, so I was very grateful, maybe not at their methods, but it got the job done.

I loved school, but after several months, it finally took a terrible toll on me. I was exhausted and living on pure nerves and "wake-up" pills. Days went by with me forgetting to eat, and before I knew it, my clothes were falling off me from the weight loss. I was a complete mess, and it ended with me just not being able to get up and go to school at all.

The showers no longer worked. I knew that the water was covering me, but I really couldn't feel it. My grades were good except for the odd falling asleep during class, but it became official when the school sent me a notice saying that "our current situation was not working" and if I wanted to get through school, my only recourse would be to get my GED.

I really missed the classes I was taking in law and politics. At the time, I thought that it could possibly be a positive career path. Having to leave school was terribly emotional, so I concentrated on my work and thought about how to get my GED.

I had been thinking about my mom a lot lately and decided to call her. She hadn't heard from me in several months, and I knew that she constantly worried about me. When she picked up the phone, I told her that I had gone back to school, neglecting to say that I had been kicked out. She was impressed that I was taking law and wanted to become a lawyer when I finished. It was a lie I hated to tell, but I could hear her cry on the other end with pride. She asked me if I had checked my bank account lately, which I hadn't, so I told her, "No." I just took money out of the bank without looking at the balance each time I needed some money for rent, bills, or alcohol. She went on to tell me that she had been depositing money into my account for the past several months, wanting to help me out. She wished me all the success in life and told me that she would never tell my dad about any of our phone calls. She ended the call by saying how very distraught she was over my running away, but she understood why I left, and apologized emphatically for letting my father control her as much as he did. I didn't have the nerve to ask her what she actually knew about everything, so I just said a loving good-bye with a promise to call her more often.

My sister and I unfortunately started communicating again *only* because of my mother's wishes to make her happy and try to get along. Mom never knew anything of what had happened between Leanne and me, and as far as my father was concerned, he still considered me a continuous threat to him, and a disgrace to our family beyond repair. Whether the truth would ever come out, I didn't care; I was finally free.

The psychiatrist tried to convince me that what Leanne had done was out of pure jealousy and that eventually it would be exposed. I held onto that thought, and it killed me inside trying to get along with such a horrible, demonic bitch, but I loved Mom more than anything, so I did try fighting the trepidation whenever I had to see or speak to her, making sure those memories never came up in conversation.

Leanne had done too many horrific things to me that it would have killed Mom if she knew, so I made the effort, against my better judgment, knowing what Leanne was capable of doing, if I did. With all I had been through with her, her demonic aggression actually scared me, and I knew that the more I saw her, the more she would try to destroy me.

CHAPTER 19

I made a decision to evolve past the life I once lived and had met a wonderful woman, Debbie, at the watering hole I frequented. I ended up drinking with her many evenings, and was surprised at how she could pack away the alcohol. She had just left her live-in boyfriend, Jim, and since we had started such a great relationship, we decided to try to find a house we could rent together.

Debbie had a civil servant job and was very intelligent. She was definitely straight, and I thought this would be a brand-new start for the both of us. She found a cute two-bedroom bungalow to rent right in the core of downtown Toronto, close to Sherbourne and Bloor. It was perfect for the two of us and affordable. It worked out well, being a stone's throw to the liquor store right behind the house, and we both had become quite the seasoned drinkers with the occasional street drug to help us forget our pasts. In a panic, I quit Bittner's Deli when my boss finally insisted on seeing my SIN card. I always tried to avoid confrontations whenever possible, and I didn't want to get yelled at for causing him trouble with the law or his superiors, so I just left. I was still underage and wanted it kept a secret from everyone.

My credit cards were maxed out with the rent due, and Bittner's was only paying enough just to get by. My mom's money was slowly depleting from my account, so I headed to the Gasworks bar to contemplate my next move. It was then that I met two men celebrating the first-year anniversary of their business, and I bumped into one of them on the way to the washroom. He invited me for a drink at their table, and they looked safe enough in their high-priced three-piece suits, so I joined them. The conversation was mostly about me, and after I told them that I had just quit my job, Max and Mark shared a glance before offering me a job at their studio, where I could make enough money to live anywhere I wanted in Toronto. That definitely got my attention, so when I asked about the job, I was told that it was just a receptionist position with very easy money.

I didn't quite understand what he was talking about, but we met a few times over the next week. He and Mark convinced me to come on board, and once I learned the job, they would move me up to management. I assumed that the business probably wasn't legal, but I was tired of being broke. When they took me out to a very expensive restaurant the next evening, we had the best champagne and food that money could buy. They reeked of money and business experience, and it made me want that skill as well. I finally agreed and was looking forward to my next adventure in life. I had nothing left to lose at that point, and I was excited at the prospect.

After we finished dinner, I agreed to meet them at their business called Venus Health Studios, which was north of the city on Yonge Street in Toronto. I wasn't exactly sure what a health studio was, but as I walked up the steep staircase to the second floor, I decided that I would take the job regardless of what the business was.

Venus Health Studios apparently was a massage parlor, and I heard that Mel Lastman, the mayor of Toronto, had been determined to close them down. When I voiced my concerns to Mark and Max, they told me that Venus was for massages only and nothing more. I certainly did not want to get arrested for anything bad, so, I agreed to be the receptionist there and not one of the masseuses.

I would be overseeing four women there, and I was warned that they would lie, cheat, and steal if I wasn't constantly on guard watching them. They weren't present the night we arrived, which I thought a little weird, but I didn't care. Apparently, the studio was closed that evening, but should those women have been there, I would have understood what was going on, and maybe thought twice about taking the job.

When I did meet these girls, they were sleazy, wearing the most provocative clothing or should I say, the very least clothing possible with gartered stockings and stiletto shoes. I'm guessing that Max had a pep talk with them prior to me coming and instructed them not to tell me what they were really doing with the men in the privacy of their rooms. They kept to themselves, and we didn't communicate much except for the money that they gave me at the end of each shift when we closed.

During the first week, I had made $1,750, which back in the seventies was an amazing salary for a 7-hour shift working Wednesday through Sunday, and I was really happy with my decision to work there. Eventually, the girls and I started getting along very well, and they began to open up to me about what they actually did with their men.

The massages would begin with them both having a shower together and then going into their separate rooms for the massage. The unspoken fees I later found out were that a BJ was $50, full sex was $100, and "around the world" was $150 for the hour, plus tips. Now I understood why I received so much money; getting a percentage of what the girls made as well as my receptionist rate of $50 per hour.

This went on for several months until two of the girls decided to leave and go elsewhere. Business had seriously picked up, and then Max came in to speak to me about becoming more than just a receptionist. I was told that if I continued to work reception as well as doing massages I could make a lot more money, but how much I wasn't sure until I agreed to do it. Of course, my boundaries were shaky at best from my childhood, but Max accepted the limited ones I gave. There were also warnings that undercover cops would try to come in and bust us for prostitution, but Max knew I had the smarts to spot those cops if they tried.

Max was right about me making a hell of a lot more money. I was pulling in $1,000 most nights with the massages taking me less than an hour to do. I was good at what I did, but I was also disgusted because of my history with these kinds of pigs. I did love the money and having such a luxurious lifestyle with furs, jewelry, and enough money that I could occasionally go to the Gasworks and buy the entire bar a round of drinks. I knew it wouldn't last, so I took full advantage of it and lived a life I never dreamed was possible.

The cops were coming in almost every night, but I got to recognize them instantly. I would send them to the shower by themselves and cover their privates while they lay on the massage table, and when they tried to touch me, I nicely told them that I was flattered but what they wanted was against the rules, and if they continued, they would have to leave with no refund.

The cops were easy to spot and stuck out like a headless horse. They were really nice to me, but I could always tell who they were. Of course, while they showered, I would go through their pockets to find their badges, which helped in identifying the ones I didn't happen to date. As they left, three out of five would ask me for my phone number, and I would innocently give it to them. It was the beginning of a beautiful friendship with Toronto's finest.

I actually did date a few of them when they invited me out to their popular cop bar, mainly just to get information about the laws and memorize their faces should one slip by me at the parlor. On my days off, Max would work the desk, but being a man, he wasn't as clued in with the faces as I was, and on the nights he worked, I would go in the next day to find that the place was busted up and so was Max. He either had a broken arm or ribs or his face was badly bruised, so he extended my hours to cover seven days a week, and it was exhausting. I was working 11:00 p.m. to 5:00 a.m. Monday to Friday and 5:00 p.m.to 5:00 a.m. on weekends.

I didn't experience too many perverted

trouble-making creeps coming in, and I always kept my can of pepper spray taped under my desk in case I needed it. I only had to use it twice, and I was thankful that I had it. There was only one time that it didn't work. Some creep came in hyped up on PCP with such an aggressive attack that caught me off-guard, and I couldn't see it coming. He tried to destroy the studio, and of course, I couldn't call the cops, so I just flirted with him calmly, telling him that I would take very good care of him. As he settled down, my fist went fast and hard to his throat and my stilettos went into his groin. He hit the floor moaning. My baseball bat was never far out of my reach, and as he lay there, I gave him a choice, standing over him with the bat ready to swing. He took the hint and dragged himself out of the studio on his belly with me locking the door behind him. I called Max immediately, and he showed up within minutes with his thirty-eight caliber handgun drawn and ready to use in case the guy came back with reinforcements.

I threw my money around like it was water. I had all the materialistic things I could ever want, but again, I knew that this job wasn't going to last forever. It was fun making so much money whether it was legal or not, and the entire downtown crowd knew me. For once, I was the most popular person in town. I thought it might be the life I wanted until we were robbed one night at the house while Debbie and I were sleeping. Someone broke into our house and stole all my jewelry and furs, probably going undetected because of the cocaine coma we were in from the previous two days, and with me getting through my long hours at work.

I asked around and actually found the bastard was who robbed us. Apparently, he worked at a strip club not far from the Gasworks, so I went to the club to confront him. He was the bouncer there and one of the largest men I had ever seen. Standing next to him, I came up to his waist, and he had to be over 350 pounds. "What the fuck do you want?" he asked as I approached him. I could see one of the jeweled rings on his finger I had bought for a recent relationship gone bad, and of course, he denied it. He told me to get the hell away from his bar or the next time he would put a bullet in my brain. I left and took the loss, but I learned a lot from the experience.

Debbie and I lived together for two years while I worked at Venus, and we had a great time before she decided to move back with her abusive boyfriend. We were so much alike that we could have been sisters, and I often wished that we were, instead of having Leanne. I didn't want to keep the house myself when she moved out, so I had to find an apartment, and probably another job close by that I could walk to. The cops were getting better at what they were doing at the parlors, and I was getting very antsy, unable to identify them like I used to, so it was just a question of time before they busted me.

At the same time, I had spoken to my sister, who mentioned that her friend was getting married and wanted to quit her job. She had been working for a good company as an executive secretary, and was now looking for a replacement. I asked her to mention me to her, whom she did, and within two weeks, I was the new executive secretary to the president of a well-known Toronto company. I was there several months thinking that it wasn't anything that I thought it would be; typing up membership cards, mailing labels, sending the odd letter, and not much else. I couldn't take the boredom any longer, so after a couple of months, it was time to leave.

CHAPTER 20

Going to Vancouver had always been on my mind, and now the time had come. I decided to give two week's notice and take the train west to Vancouver. My boss said that he would lay me off so I could collect unemployment that would cover me once I arrived.

My back had gotten a lot worse, and my right shoulder had protruded significantly with excruciating pain. I was still living in my downtown house while working, but decided the house had to go too. I sold everything inside within the two weeks and bought a one-way ticket to Vancouver. I was very excited but had little money left and nowhere to go once I got there. Unemployment insurance would kick in shortly, so I knew at least I would have some money until I got a job.

My last day came, and I said good-bye to the few people I knew or cared about. They thought I was crazy doing something so frivolous, but I got onto the train with one suitcase and then it finally hit me with what I was doing. I just didn't care. It was a three-day ride to Vancouver in coach, which wasn't the most comfortable. I started receiving unemployment, which would transfer out to Vancouver once I had an address for them to send the check to, so I had to find a place fast. I made friends with everyone on the train, and that included the train's conductors and stewards.

Dancing, nursing, and becoming a cop were the only three careers that I ever wanted to do. I knew that my spine disease would prevent me from ever becoming a cop, which I had a great aptitude for with all my experience, and I loved the hype. I knew in my heart that it was not going to happen, so I started to consider my other options.

My attempt at dancing was a failure. When I was younger, I begged my mom to put me into a jazz dance class. Unfortunately, I wasn't able to do many of the routines because of my spine, and I wasn't able to bend like the rest of the class, so that was out of the question, and I was asked to leave.

Nursing, however, was available at the University of British Columbia, and I could apply as a mature student, take their entrance exam, and become a nurse. That intrigued me to no end, so I became fixated on that goal.

Halfway to Vancouver, I met a steward on the

train named Carl and spent a lot of time with him. When I told him that I had nowhere to go once I got to Vancouver, he offered me a room in his uncle's home, where he spent his layovers. At least I now had a place I could stay until I could get my bearings and find an affordable room.

When we pulled into the station, I waited outside for Carl to finish his job before the train went into service. He told me that he had already called his uncle and they were happy that he was bringing a friend home. Carl was somewhat of a loner, not a handsome man, and very quiet. In my opinion, he had never dated once in his twenty-three years. I didn't want anyone to get the wrong idea, so I kept my distance while we drove to their house. It was a gorgeous ranch bungalow located at the base of the mountain. The view was amazing, and I knew then that Vancouver was going to be my new home forever. There were also three thousand miles separating me from my family and enough space between us to make me feel safe, and I smiled at the thought.

Within the first week, I found a room in a house, but the landlord was a really strange man. I didn't care because the rent was cheap, and it was local to just about everything downtown. I hadn't gotten to the university yet because I was too busy looking for a job. I was drawn to Arbutus Street, where there was a long-term care home. I took my resumé inside looking for the boss. She was very impressed with my résumé although it was exaggerated with several references from Toronto. I figured that with the distance between us and time difference she was less likely to verify them.

She was a handsome woman and very overweight, but she was an experienced nurse and had been at the home for several years. When I told her that I was excited to become a nurse, she explained that her home was affiliated with the university and that I could be taught there at her home and be certified as a registered nurse's assistant when I finished. I would have to complete the programs and write the exam mandated by the university, but when I finished in two years, I would have achieved my goal of becoming a nurse. I smiled and said, "I can start tomorrow." We shook hands, and now I finally had a real honest purpose in life.

I called my parents collect that night and told them I had moved to Vancouver. I spoke to my mom, who was thrilled with my plans, and then my father got on the phone and started belittling and degrading me to the point that I had to make him stop. Being so far away from his grasp, there was nothing he could do to me here, or so I thought. I started getting snippy with him the same way he was with me, and when he asked me my plans, I told him that I was joining the French Foreign Legion and was shipping out soon to Europe. There was silence on the phone, so I knew that I had gotten him good with that one. I didn't even know what the French Foreign Legion was and had only heard something about it the day before listening to some random person in a café talking about it. I wasn't paying much attention at the time, but it seemed to work on my father.

I was doing very well at work and loving the knowledge that would bring me closer to my dream. I had registered at the university after passing my entrance exam and was enjoying the beauty that Vancouver had to offer; the mountains, ocean, and campus at UBC. I made a few friends there in such a short time and then got invited to a party in Kitsilano by someone in my class. I was thrilled that people liked me for myself, so on Friday night after work, I headed to the address I was given. It was an amazing house close to the campus, surrounded by gorgeous trees and close to the beach.

Apparently, Vancouver students took their partying very seriously with huge speakers at every corner of the house, which I noticed right away. There was no furniture on the main floor, and I was told that it was the dance area with hardwood floors and heavy blinds on the windows to dull the loud music that was blasting through the house as I entered.

Jim, one of the owners, asked if I wanted a tour of the house, and with a nod, we headed to the basement. There were five people who shared the house, all students at the university. Their careers included law, medicine, politics, and paleontology, with one amazing guy who was going through to become a thoracic surgeon. These were incredible people with the drive to succeed in life, and I felt very blessed just to be invited to their party. These were the kinds of people I wanted to insert into my life, and I would do what it took to be a part of their group. I was finally on the upswing of life, and the adrenaline was pumping through my veins, loving every minute of it.

As we entered the basement, I noticed it wasn't finished but then we rounded the corner, and I could see five mattresses thrown onto the floor with dressers and coat racks where their clothes hung at each bed. When I asked, he told me that this was where everyone slept. It was a party house for sure, and I loved the ambiance and awesome world they had created for themselves.

It was maybe midnight when I left to catch the last bus home. I stood at the bus stop for what seemed like hours when a car pulled up beside me. I recognized the guy from the party, and he asked if I wanted a lift home. I appreciated the offer but told him that I would wait for the bus. He smiled at my response and told me that it would be a very long wait because the buses had finished running for the night. I graciously accepted his offer and got into the car.

His name was Paul, and he was drop-dead gorgeous. He was the soon-to-be thoracic surgeon I had met at the party. He carried the conversation the entire time with his ambitions to become the best surgeon in Canada, and I was very impressed. My worries about accepting a ride from a stranger quickly lifted as we drove to my place, and he let me out. As I was leaving the car, he reached over, touching my arm, and asked what I was doing the following Saturday, or if I was working. When I replied that it was my day off, he told me that a bunch of his friends were going to "Wreck Beach" and asked if I wanted to tag along with them. Although I wasn't familiar with that beach, I loved the idea of being with these same people again, so I agreed to go. Now that he knew my address, he told me that he would pick me up at eleven that morning and all I needed was a towel. They would bring the beer and smokes. He ended by saying that bathing suits were optional and then drove off.

I thought it was wonderful just to be invited, and after waking up a few hours later, still hazy from the alcohol, I made my way to work. I felt great even through the haze. I was making friends and starting the kind of life that I had always wanted in a city I had taken a big chance on, and I was so glad I did. I was finally happy!

Wreck Beach was something I didn't expect. It was a nude beach, and to get to it, you had to climb down a ninety-degree slope of deep sand. As we got to the bottom, I looked up to see a few uniformed officers standing at the top, ordering us to leave because what we were doing was illegal. The several men and women with their families who were already there just flipped off the cops with a joking glare and no fear whatsoever.

Paul noticed the concern on my face and reassured me that for years he had been coming to this beach with no problems. The cops wouldn't attempt the hill, possibly because of the enormous slope or the deep sand that would dirty their uniforms in the process; he wasn't sure. He went on to say that families came from all over Canada to enjoy this beach, with many families actually sewing their clothes together to make tents and staying there for weeks with their kids as a family vacation in the nude. There had never been any real trouble to speak of, so the cops didn't really care and stood at the top of the hill, bellowing out threats just to show their presence.

Everything was going well at work, and I was gaining the experience and credits to finally become a nurse. A few days had passed since the beach, and after work, I always took a walk through the main street leading to my house. This day was very different though; I had the feeling that I was being followed. It was a dreadful feeling, and several times, I quickly turned around to check if anyone stood out.

Throughout the week that followed, I was still disturbed that someone was watching my every move. Instead of turning impulsively to find no one there, I paused to look into a shop window that reflected everything on the street. It was then that I could see the same man hiding behind a parked car, spying on me in a bizarre way while snapping pictures of me. I began walking faster, and as I picked up the pace, I could see that he had done the same. I wasn't sure what to do, so I headed home as quickly as I could. After I turned the corner on my street, I ran as fast as I could so he wouldn't see where I lived.

I loved writing poetry and usually did it outside my window on the roof nearly every night. I had privacy there to write the words I actually wanted to say and that made me feel good about me. As I was looking down in deep thought, I could see this same man again getting into his car opposite the house. I was terrified that he had found me and started shouting obscenities that ended with my threats to call the police. He immediately got into his car after shooting another picture and then took off at high speed. I crawled back into my window and considered the police, but the last thing I wanted was the police getting involved. There was no reason for this man to be following me, unless he was somehow affiliated with my demented father, recalling my telephone conversation with him. Our family secrets were a thing of the past now thank God, and I would do anything I could not to have those memories dug up again, when everything was going so well for me.

I lay on my bed overpowered with back pain, so I smoked a joint and somehow fell into a deep and comforting sleep. I woke up with the sun shining through my window and the birds chirping in the crisp autumn air. The mountains in the background relaxed me and separated me from my thoughts. It was the first twenty seconds I loved each morning before reality set in, until my mind would race with everything I wanted to forget.

I showered and dressed in my nurse's outfit, ready for my walk to work. I must have looked paranoid with the twisting and turning I did on the street, searching for this guy I knew nothing about. When I got to work, I tried desperately to do the job I was being paid to do. My boss was amazing, but she noticed the difference in me at once. She pulled me into her office, concerned with my behavior.

I told her the whole sordid story about this creep and how frightened I was. When she asked if I recognized him, I told her that I had never seen him before he appeared the week prior. She reassured me that she would double the security at work and suggested I walk home with a friend. I felt a bit relieved, but I certainly wasn't going to scare away my great new friends by asking them to pick me up and drive me home. She suggested that I call the police, but with my experience with cops, it felt better not having them involved. Although she couldn't understand my apprehension, she just nodded and sent me back to my floor.

CHAPTER 21

I was working the late shift, and it was dark when I left work, but as I walked out the door, I suspiciously searched both ways before heading home. From out of nowhere, this creep jumped out of an alley and grabbed me. When I tried to scream, he covered my mouth with duct tape and dragged me further from the street. He still hadn't identified himself but then handcuffed me and quickly placed a burlap bag over my head with little room to breathe. He threw me into the back-seat of what I thought was the same car I saw him parked in on my street the night before. I was terrified but helpless with the bag and handcuffs making me unable to fight him off. Before he slammed the door shut, I managed to knee him in his groin, but he hit me over the head with some heavy object until I blacked out. When I woke up later in the car, the blood was warm as it continued to trickle down from my head.

I couldn't see whether it was day or night, but

I could feel the road beneath us and knew that we were traveling at high speeds; probably on some kind of highway. There must have been a defect in one of the tire treads, because they made a specific click as they rotated, and I started counting them as we drove. When I reached a thousand, I blacked out again with the trickle of blood now running down into my mouth. It was as if the horror of a familiar past was happening to me all over again, but I pushed aside the idea that this was somehow related to my father; surely because the huge geographical distance between us was enough to feel safe.

I was hungry and thirsty, starving for not only food but for information as to what was happening to me and where we were going. Through the tape on my mouth, which had loosened from the sweat, I managed to call out and ask what was going on. I demanded him to tell me what the hell was happening, where we were going, and who was responsible for me being there? There was no answer except for his command to, "shut up and stay quiet," and another familiarity I was now starting to reconsider. My mind was racing with what to do next. My cuffed wrists had started to hurt being behind my back, giving me such horrendous pain that I started to scream for help.

I could feel the car pull over and the front door closing as the back door opened. I honestly thought that he was going to kill me, so I stopped screaming. Maybe it would be best if he just put a bullet into my head now to end it all. The unknown fear was rapidly growing. I was belligerent toward him, until he spoke telling me that if I was a good girl, he would put my hands to the front and would stop to get me some food at the next McDonalds' restaurant.

I promised, thinking that I might have a chance to escape, or he would at least tell me what was going on, where we were going, and if he was going to rape and kill me. He just laughed at my suffering, telling me that he was sorry but things would change for the better soon. It was another familiarity I recognized, but wasn't sure! Then he told me that we were headed back to Ontario and that it would be a nice surprise when we got there. He also added that he had no intentions of raping or killing me. I couldn't think of any surprise that was good enough to go back to Ontario for, but now I knew that my father was somehow responsible for all this. I frantically blurted out with the hope that he would listen to me that if he was taking me back to my parents, my father would rape me again and possibly try to kill me, *again*. My life was in Vancouver now, and it was a great life I had created for myself, away from that bastard who had ruined my childhood.

When we pulled over, I thought that he would hurt me again, so I kept quiet. I was surprised shortly after we stopped when the door opened, and I could smell food. I wolfed down the food he had given me through the hole in the bag on my face he cut out, and the Coke he had given me that made me want more. I heard the car door close after he told me to lie back down on the seat and enjoy the rest of the ride. I never thought I would survive another few days with the pain and constant fear, but I remembered my doctor saying that there were two types of people; survivors and victims', and with all that I had gone through in my life, I refused to be the latter.

He must have put some kind of drug in my Coke because I passed out soon after drinking it. When I woke up, I had no idea whether it was day or night, and when I tried to speak, I heard my words slur as if I were drunk.

"Where are we now?" I asked calmly. "We're in Saskatchewan," he replied. I automatically thought of the Moose Jaw Motel with the memories of Sharon and me flowing through my mind. I begged him to stop for a good night's rest and promised to be good if he did, knowing the manager there would help me. He refused, saying that we had just passed it and we had to get to our destination on time. I kept begging him until he pulled over onto the shoulder. The bag was still on my head. Instead, he gave me another pop from a can this time. I was so thirsty I drank it as quickly as it was given. It tasted a little tart, but it felt great going down my throat. He quickly re-taped my mouth as we pulled off the shoulder and back onto the highway. I soon started to feel the effects of the drug in the Coke, falling back asleep before finishing my sentence.

When I finally woke up, he had announced that we were almost at our destination and that he had a great surprise for me. Anything was better than this, but if we were heading east to Ontario, the only people there, were the monsters I ran away from. I knew I had to do something, but I was hazy from the drugs, my hands were cuffed, and my mouth still taped with the burlap bag over my head. I was out of options.

I lay silently while another hour passed before we finally stopped again, and I was ushered out of the car. I was placed on what seemed to be a cement surface and told to stay put for five minutes before removing the burlap bag from my head. The horn blew twice before I heard him drive off, and I knew that this would be my only chance to escape. I slowly turned in the direction of the car and carefully calculated each step down a sloped surface, struggling to get the bag off.

Then I heard what seemed like a door opening, and soon after, my mother removing the bag. I was so pissed off that the life I had made for myself in Vancouver was totally ruined and I would never get that back again. The contract at the long term care facility where I worked specifically stated that if anyone was absent from any shift and didn't call that they would be fired immediately. My classes at the university were very intense, and I had now missed my term exam while on this safari. Without a reasonable explanation, I would automatically fail the course, and lose my job. When I registered for my classes, I was advised upon signing up, that it was a privilege to attend their programs, and that they would not tolerate any carelessness on my part.

I was angrier than I thought I ever could be after mom removed the burlap bag. She cuddled me in her arms, telling me how happy she was to have me home, and how sorry she was for the way it had been done.

"What the hell is going on here," I asked, "and how could you be party to such a thing Mom?" screaming at her for an answer. The blood had finally dried, but with my head being under the bag for so long, it had covered my entire face. "Look at me!" "What about this looks anything less than evil and crazy?" I continued screaming. "How the hell could you let him talk you into this?"

Mom was crying hysterically, clipping off the plastic ties that bound my hands, and then I heard his voice as he approached. He used that gruff-like threatening voice I used to fear so much. As she held the bag with my hands now freed, I could see her trying to hold me in her arms. I pushed her away with contempt written all over my face, and she stepped back, shocked that I would do such a thing.

Then the bastard spoke as if he was the king of my life. As I listened, I could tell that he was solely responsible for this nightmare I never thought he was even capable of doing. He always could manipulate my mother into helping him with his cruel plans because she was such a weakling. Part of me understood why, but for her to do this to someone she claimed to love was beyond my comprehension. Dad ushered me into the kitchen away from any witnesses who could have been watching us on the street. I was told to sit on the chair with the meal my mother placed in front of me, just staring at the spaghetti on the plate. Was there no other food in the world to serve but spaghetti? I was so hungry that I devoured the food in silence just the same. It was the only real home-cooked meal I had had for the past four days, but I needed to prepare myself for the worst when I finished. My eyes were glued on my father, sitting across from me with those dark satanic eyes, and that too familiar fear I always faced prior to his attacks.

When I finished, he pulled his chair up beside me now within arm's reach of me, while I wondered what he would do to me next. He was uncomfortably calm, but that was his MO until he would lash out at me. I prepared myself with my hands held tight and steady above the table; ready to protect myself against the first blow I knew was coming.

Again, he had ushered Mom out of the kitchen, sending her to her room, and another familiar command we were both used to, watching her reluctantly leave. I heard those squeaking stairs I always tried to avoid coming home late at night as she climbed them.

He folded his hands in his lap, contemplating his next move I'm sure. Instead, he was too calm and cool for me to read, and it frightened me. Then, he started to say that he loved me very much, that he wasn't fooled by our phone conversation when I told him that I was joining the French Foreign Legion. He looked me straight in my eyes and told me that he couldn't allow that to happen. I must have looked confused because I still had no idea of what that fight or war was about.

When I asked, he explained that they were some kind of military cult who fought and died for the wrong reasons and it would eventually get me killed. I laughed out loud, telling him that the only reason I told him that was to hurt him, and I had no intentions of joining any group I knew nothing about. When I told him about my life in Vancouver and the RNA degree I was working toward, he looked as if he didn't believe me because of course I was too stupid and incapable of getting such a degree. He stood up, shaking his head, saying that nothing had changed and I was still the pathological liar he claimed me to be.

Now, I was raging mad and reminded him that he was the master of lies. He was the inhumane one, not to mention disgusting with what he had done to me as a child, and something only a person who was mentally deranged could possibly do. I gave him the name of the home and my boss he could call for verification, but I could see he wasn't going to call anyone who could prove I was telling the truth. He cut me short of finishing my sentence and went on to tell me that he had hired a private detective to kidnap me and bring me home so that I wouldn't die just to spite him, and hopefully, I would come to my senses. I was furious at what he had done; ruining my only opportunity of fulfilling my dream in a life that I would have done anything to pursue. What an asshole he was for destroying my chance to become someone successful.

Things did start to make a lot of sense with that hired jackass who was stalking, trapping, and kidnapping me in Vancouver. The thing that bugged me the most was that my gut told me my father had something to do with it, and I dismissed it as not being remotely possible. I wouldn't let that happen again!

There was silence for a few minutes until I got up from the table, put my dish in the sink, and headed upstairs to my bedroom. I really thought that I had actually left him thinking about what he had done, but my back was horrifically painful, and I needed to lie down on my bed before heading to the shower I desperately needed. Whatever was going on could wait until the morning, and I told him to go to hell before leaving the kitchen.

My bed felt great after being tied up in the backseat of an economy car with no room to stretch my legs. I must have fallen asleep because I woke up with the sun shining in my window and my mother affectionately sitting beside me on the bed, staring at me while I slept.

She had heard most of the conversation from the top of the stairs, listening the way I used to do all those years. Then she told me how sorry she was for allowing dad to talk her into doing this to me. She went on to say that they both thought I was really going to join the French Foreign Legion, and with everything that dad had told her about them, she was terrified I would be killed while fighting a war I had no right to be fighting.

CHAPTER 22

It felt so good to have her arms around me again, but my back pain was so intolerable that I couldn't help but contort uncontrollably. She noticed it right away, and as I sat up, she could see the growth on the right side of my shoulder. It had protruded terribly since she saw me last, and that scared her. The following day, she would take me to see our family doctor and get some x-rays of my spine, remembering the hell my sister went through prior to her surgery. For the first time, she actually saw in me the same thing she had seen in my sister with the deformation, and she apologized for ignoring me the way she had done for so many years.

Mom kept her word and took me to the doctor's office first thing in the morning. He wrote a script for pain meds and a requisition for the x-ray, which we went to immediately after the appointment. We had to wait two weeks for the doctor to get the results, but when he did, he actually called us himself, and my mother nearly dropped the phone, listening as he spoke.

I was born with this terrible disease, and my spine had grown to a 49 percent deviation in the form of an "s." It protruded into my shoulder as well as inward, compromising the growth of my right lung. I needed surgery badly, or it would only get worse. He continued to tell her that he was referring me to a surgeon at St. Michael's hospital in downtown Toronto but warned that it could be awhile before the appointment. In his opinion, this surgeon was one of the best spine surgeons in Canada. Mom was freaked out, remembering my sister, the "Stryker Frame", and how Leanne had fallen out of it when that huge wheel turned her over. The doctor assured her that the medical profession had progressed over the years and pleaded with her to take me to the appointment. Mom agreed, and four months later, we entered the surgeon's office.

While waiting for my appointment, mom was constantly fighting with dad, hating him for ignoring me through all those years I constantly complained of the pain in my chest and back, and then, doing nothing about it. The disease was growing inside me, and mom was horrified knowing that her only other daughter was suffering so terribly with the same disease.

Apparently, my father's mother had the same

spine problem, so it was hereditary, but that was way back when they knew nothing about Scoliosis. When she was younger, she was always hunched over and complaining about some kind of terrible pain in her back, neck, and arms. None of her children believed in her complaints because she was a hypochondriac, so the family would just give her the attention they believed she wanted, soothing her like a "baby needing its pacifier," and dismissed all of her symptoms and complaints.

After the surgeon received the results from my x-rays, I was scared to death of the prognosis, but mom was always right beside me with a positive word that everything was going to be okay. It was reassuring, but that was my mom. She was always easy to read with her fears clearly showing all over her face.

When the surgeon returned to the room, his tone was calm and his posture straight as he tried to explain that with my spine having a 49 percent deviation; it required a surgical procedure that would take several hours to complete because of its complexity. He would break my spine in two places, stretching it approximately four inches; the extent of the curvature. He was optimistic that the surgery would be successful and the hump on my back would also disappear completely. Should we choose to leave it any longer would be catastrophic, and at age 21, my health as an adult would be severely compromised, and the damage could possibly be irreversible. He continued on to say how intricate the spine was with so many nerves and muscles involved, but I stopped him when I noticed my Mom wasn't listening anymore.

Mom had already started to cry, cussing under her breath that she had listened to my dad all this time, convincing her that I was just trying to get attention. In between sobs, she spoke out about my sister and the hell that she had endured with the Stryker Frame. The surgeon looked at her sympathetically, explaining that medical advancements had come a long way since then, and he felt confident that I would actually be the first patient to be put into a bed instead of the Stryker Frame, making for a quicker recovery. That was somewhat comforting, but he also had to give the five percent possibility that I could die on the operating table due to complications with such a convoluted surgical procedure.

Nonetheless, the surgery was set for October 15 and four months prior to my twenty-first birthday. That would be a little over a year away, only because children's bodies stop growing by then. That meant I would still have to suffer the same horrific pain until then. My mom was insistent in telling the doctor how much pain I was in, and was somewhat relieved when he brought out his prescription pad, telling her that the pain medication he was giving was stronger and would help me until then.

I was too weak to argue, knowing that I had to spend the next year with my parents again. I wasn't about to do that but didn't have the heart to tell my mom. Living another year of a hell I once survived was not an option for me now or anytime in the future, but we drove back home just the same. It was a long and silent drive back to the suburbs where we lived, so far from my downtown life, which, as dangerous as downtown was, it was so much better than living at home. My mind was racing with how I could get through yet another year in pain before surgery; where I would live until then, and how I would find a job I desperately needed to keep my mind off the pain.

The next few weeks were unbearable, so I started considering my options. I decided to move out to an apartment I found in St. James Town; a highly populated area in the heart of downtown, consisting of several buildings that encompassed a four-block radius, housing more than five hundred thousand residents. I landed a job at an insurance company that would only require one subway to get to work, so I grabbed it. It was a far cry from becoming a nurse, but with surgery coming up, I just needed something as easy as a file clerk position until then.

Meanwhile, my relationship with Kathy was

going strong again. She was a beautiful brunette with such a great outgoing personality. While I was gone, she did have a son but had adopted him out, and I considered that it was Roger's baby but was afraid to ask. Meanwhile, her relationship with Roger had become very stressed; finding out that he was cheating on her with other women when he wasn't home, or he'd be so drunk he would have to crawl home, passing out in her apartment hallway until it finally got her evicted.

Roger was part Cherokee Indian so drinking was part of his heritage, and we all accepted that. Kathy, Roger, and I had gone out often together to the local bars, and even though I felt like a third wheel many times, I was still popular with the many men who were attracted to me. I was very lonely, and just wanted to meet someone sincere and really nice. Someone I could have a relationship with that would develop into something long-term, and hopefully, take me away from everything bad in my life.

CHAPTER 23

I was settled into my new apartment after a month of shopping at second-hand stores for furniture that my mother paid for, but the people who lived in the building were really weird. Again, this was downtown living, and I accepted it without judgment.

After one night staying late at work, I got home and made myself something to eat. At eleven p.m. I was tired and headed to the bedroom. I had almost dozed off when I heard my buzzer with someone in the lobby trying very hard to get me to answer. As I pushed the intercom button, I found that it was Roger, who sounded drunk. He needed me to buzz him up, so I got dressed and waited for him at the door. It was almost an hour before he arrived, and when I opened the door, Roger was completely covered with blood from head to toe. I quickly scanned the hall for anyone who may have seen him and then quickly pulled him into my apartment, demanding to know what had happened.

Roger said he had met some guy at my door trying to get in. This had been a regular occurrence for me, and being right across from the stairwell didn't help. Every time I heard a knock at my door, I'd look through the peep-hole, opening the door to find no one there.

After several days, it started to totally freak me out, and it continued even when I had friends over for the evening. The music may have been a little loud, but I always heard the knock, and again, no one was there when I opened the door. Friends would tell me that I was being paranoid because they never heard anything. The one thing they couldn't explain was after each knock, I'd write a derogatory note and slip it under the door, telling whoever was there to "go screw him or her and to leave me alone." When my friends were leaving to go home, the note had mysteriously disappeared and was nowhere to be found in the hall or the stairway.

When Roger arrived at my apartment, he said he met this guy standing at my door, offering to flip a coin to see who would "fuck" me first. Roger, in his usually drunken state, was disgusted, and immediately suggested that they go down to the sub-basement to discuss the situation, and that was the reason it took him so long to finally arrive at my door.

When he finished his story, he insisted that I go downstairs with him to the sub-basement to see if I recognized the guy. Why this person would still be downstairs was beyond me, and then I realized that they must have had a terrible fight and the guy was badly hurt. I grabbed my keys and slammed the door shut behind us. I ran toward the elevator while Roger lagged behind, telling me that the guy wasn't going anywhere in his condition. The elevator took forever until we finally arrived.

When the elevator door opened, I could see the man lying with his back toward me and his hand running down the wall, covered in blood and leaving a trail of bloody finger-prints as they slowly slid down to the floor. The man was dressed in a suit that looked very familiar, and as my mind raced trying to figure out where I had seen it before, I realized that it looked very much like the suit Dave used to wear when he went to work. I couldn't help but scream at what was happening, and then I saw his teeth lying beside him in a pool of blood. I thought Roger had knocked his jaw completely out of his face but couldn't tell with so much blood present. I cried Dave's name, but Roger calmly said it wasn't him.

I immediately ran back upstairs to my apartment and called both Dave and then an ambulance. Thank God Dave answered on the second ring. I told him quickly in a panic what had happened and that the police were on their way with an ambulance. I insisted that he come as soon as possible to get Roger out of there so he wouldn't be arrested for attempted murder, or worse. With Dave living only a couple of streets over, he arrived in rapid time before the cops. I could hear the sirens from my balcony, so Dave grabbed Roger and dragged him out of my apartment through the back of the building and took him back to his place.

It was a minute or two later when the cops buzzed me from the lobby and arrived at my apartment door with guns drawn. As I let them in, I was still frantic, telling them that I was doing my laundry in the sub-basement when I found that man lying there, terrified that he was dead. I continued to tell them that I didn't have much more information than that, only that they needed to get down there quickly to save his life. One of the cops used his radio to instruct the ambulance to meet them there as soon as possible.

I escorted the officers to where I saw the man last, and as the elevator door opened, the man was still there moaning and making a terrible gurgling sound. It was obvious that he was unable to breathe properly, but the ambulance arrived so I went back upstairs to my apartment when the phone rang. It was Dave, telling me that Roger insisted he come back to my apartment to make sure I was okay, and refused Dave's offer to change his clothes first, so, naturally, covered in blood, he was stopped by one of the cops who had the building surrounded. They grabbed him on his way up to my apartment, still drunk.

They rushed the half-dead man to the nearest hospital with a cop perched outside his door. It turned out that this guy had recently spoken to the rental office, who told him that I was a young, attractive, and single woman living in the apartment. Apparently, this jerk thought it would be a quick score and the reason he asked Roger to flip to see who would "fuck" me first.

The next day, it was all over the news, and I heard that they had arrested Roger for attempted murder if the guy had lived and murder if he died. This unnamed victim was still in intensive care, fighting for his life. Roger was still a friend and Kathy's boyfriend so I felt that I had to at least try to do something to help him.

The next day, I decided to go to the hospital to see him. I was totally shocked when I looked at him. It was a miracle that he survived, remembering the scene I saw, and with Roger's anger issues; he could have easily killed him. This man's eyes were badly bruised and swollen completely shut. Apparently, he underwent surgery for his jaw that they had to wire shut. I had never seen anything so gross and frightening in my life.

When I walked into the room, I sat beside him, trying not to vomit from the horrific damage that lay before me, and what Roger was actually capable of doing. The cop outside his door must have gone for coffee because he was nowhere to be seen. For some reason, I told the guy that I was a cop and asked him to go over his statement again with me. I listened intently while he tried to speak with his jaw wired, but I had already heard the entire story from the rental office. The man's clothes were lying on a nearby chair in an evidence bag, so I rifled through his pockets, finding the many notes I had slid under my door each time he knocked.

When I was ready to leave, I could see two huge men coming toward the room so I pulled the curtain shut and sneaked out of the room, quickly exiting via the stairwell. I called Dave as soon as I got home, and confessed to him what I had done by impersonating a police officer, and telling him what I discovered.

Dave admired me for my nerve, but there was no time to think about the trouble I could be in. The whole point of my visit was to try to help Roger, who was going to be arraigned the next day in court for attempted murder, and although he shouldn't have beat the man to an inch of his life, he was protecting me against this animal, who eventually could have raped me, if not worse. The cops weren't interested in the facts leading up to the assault; proud of themselves for catching the perpetrator as quickly as they did.

The next morning, I went to the rental office

to give them hell for what they had done to me. Candy, the agent, only shrugged and apologized for any inconvenience as if it were nothing at all, and that ticked me off. I was irate, saying that if she had never done that, this would never have happened, and she too should be arrested for conspiracy. Candy just looked at me as if I were the crazy one and told me that she had the power to evict me if I didn't stop.

"Like hell!" I yelled. "Just try it, bitch, and I will have you arrested, fired, and sue you for emotional damages!"

As I left, I threatened that this wouldn't be the last she heard of me. She didn't look too worried and back then, they didn't have the privacy laws they have today.

That evening, several of us met at the rooming house where Dave still lived, wanting to help Roger. It was then that Kathy came through the door with a fat lip and black eye. Apparently, Roger had gotten drunk before he came to my apartment and laid into her for something she never did. This was an entirely different story now, so we decided together that Roger would be on his own for this mess he had created. After several court appearances, Roger received ten years for the attempted murder, and I got evicted from my apartment with thirty days' notice.

CHAPTER 24

My boss at the insurance company was always after me for some reason, so I decided to leave and find another job. She was a total witch, and I had had enough of her insults, criticizing my wardrobe and make-up every single day. I continued to go drinking downtown at the Young Station pub and Gasworks with my friends. Cathy would meet me at my apartment, and we would walk together to the bars. Just prior to my eviction, my building decided to open up a bar in the basement, but Cathy and I just wanted to cruise for a couple of hours on our own first before meeting our friends there.

We headed down to the "Station" pub first and ordered a drink at the bar. The bartender knew us very well, so he would keep our purses behind the bar while we danced. Cathy and I were up dancing after a sip of our drinks and were having a great time with an awesome band that started playing great songs. It had to be ten minutes later when we both sat back down. We had almost finished our drinks when we started wobbling off our stools. We decided to get back up and dance the booze off, and then we both fell flat onto the dance floor.

The room was spinning when the bartender picked us both up, handing us our purses, and told us that he had called a cab for us to go home where it was safer. Something had happened, but we were too stoned to understand what was going on, when we just barely finished our first drink. When the cab arrived, I do remember two guys following close behind us, also trying to get into our cab. There was some kind of commotion instigated by the bartender behind me, dragging these two guys off us, and then telling the driver to take us right home with no stops along the way.

This new bar at my building was in full swing when we arrived in the lobby, with the best disco music only the seventy's could provide. It had to be fairly early in the evening, but we couldn't tell the difference with whatever drugs we had been given earlier. I just wanted to go upstairs to my apartment while Cathy wanted to find Dave. As the elevator opened, Dave and his friend appeared. Cathy was freaking out at Dave about something and then started slapping him across the face with no provocation. The elevator was going up, so I tried to focus on just getting to my apartment before the situation got worse. When we got to my floor, I was desperately searching for my keys. It was quite a trek to my apartment down at the end of the hall, but I felt that I had enough time to get there, unlock the door, and get in safely.

I started running to my apartment with Dave's friend close behind me. As I opened my door, I started to panic, so I headed for the kitchen to grab a pair of scissors from the drawer. It gets pretty foggy after that, but when I woke up, I found myself in bed covered in blood. Somehow, during this nightmare, I got stabbed, or so the bloody scissors lying beside me seemed to indicate.

There was no one else in my apartment, so I called for an ambulance without knowing the extent of my injuries. There was enough blood to be concerned, and I was scared that my death was imminent. I wasn't ready to die yet and thought of my mother and how she would feel if I had died from what I had created in my life. I couldn't help but blame my father for all of this; if I could have had a healthy, normal home life, then none of this would have ever happened to me. Mom, of course, had always been my strength in a strange and twisted way, so I wasn't going to let her down by dying.

When the ambulance and cops arrived, they found my front door open, and again, their guns were drawn as they cleared the apartment and entered my bedroom. The ambulance attendees examined me.

They said that it was a superficial wound and asked if I wanted to go to the hospital. The ambulance fee was really high back then, so I refused. When the cops asked me what had happened, I wasn't able to offer much information except to tell them to ask the bartender at the "Station" who saved us. Everyone finally left, and I started sobering up from the past few hours with whatever drug I was given.

I wanted to hit the rental office hard and heavy for giving out my personal information to anyone who asked, but I was still young and not even of age to fight a good battle. I also had no money for legal fees, so I just took a shower, removed the blood, and headed down to the Gasworks to have a drink or two. I was more careful now after what had just happened with the apparent date rape drug we were given. I made sure that I nursed my drink at the bar, where Kenny, the bartender, would look after me. The band had changed and wasn't the best, so I just stayed for one drink and left, walking back home.

After the thirty days came, the eviction notice forced me to leave my apartment. It was already getting close to my surgery date, so I really had no choice after I quit my job but to move back home. Mom convinced me once again that she would be there for me after surgery, and without an income, it was my only option, so I agreed.

Of course, my home life deteriorated rapidly with

my father, but he more or less left me alone; probably not attracted to me anymore sexually because of my age. He only degraded me and constantly insinuated that I wasn't worth the effort, but still claimed to love me because I was his loser daughter. I tried to understand that, but the truth was that the bastard couldn't control me anymore and knew that I could just as easily make his life as miserable as he made mine, so he backed off.

CHAPTER 25

It was now the final three-week countdown to surgery. Every night, when I lay my head down on my pillow, I kept thinking about all the terrible things I had gone through in my life. Now, I was going under the knife for a very serious operation. I was terribly deformed and kept wondering who would want me like this or even after the surgery with two feet of scars running down my back.

I was becoming very anxious and depressed, and it was getting worse by the day. Then while I was watching TV one day, a commercial came on for the "Slim Gym" exerciser I used to have that my dad threw out. This exercising machine was amazing and had me looking great in such a short time. It hooked onto a door knob connecting two ropes for your hands and feet. When you pulled your hands down, your feet went up, and it was described as the best workout you could do for ten minutes a day. It was now only $4.99, down from $29.99 from the first time I bought it, so I ordered it, and it was delivered within a couple of days.

When it came, I worked at it for two to three hours twice each day, starving myself on celery stalks and losing a ton of weight. I became anemic from the anorexia and bulimia, thinking that I could make myself so sick for the surgery that I wouldn't survive. At least if I died on the operating table, it would be a natural death. When my mother forced me to eat a meal, I would just throw it up right afterward without them knowing until it became a regular habit. I was enjoying my beautiful figure again every time I looked in the mirror.

A week before surgery, I downed a bunch of vitamins and ate as much as I needed so I would pass the pre-op test that was scheduled. After the tests, I went back to starving myself and popping several pain pills without mentioning it to anyone. I couldn't eat after midnight, the night before surgery, so I was happy that no one called to say that there were any problems with my tests. On the day of the surgery, I weighed in at 93 pounds, down from the 140 pounds I had been a month previous, and I was so anemic that when I stood up, I had to hold onto something so I wouldn't fall down. I could barely walk, but I put on a good show for my parents until we got to the hospital, and the nurse took me in immediately to an awaiting surgical bed. All I could do was pray that I would die on the operating table, working so hard the entire past weeks to ensure it would happen. I kissed my mother good-bye and told her how much I loved her as they wheeled me down the hall to prep me for surgery.

The nurse then inserted a catheter and an IV with something to relax me until they put me under with the anesthesia. I was scared, but I knew that I had a mission, and I was desperate to win. When we got to the operating room, everyone there was gowned and masked, and it freaked me out. They tied my arms down, away from my body onto metal bars so I couldn't move them. The anesthesiologist came in and told me that he was going to put me to sleep and to count back from a hundred. I don't think I got past ninety-seven before I fell asleep.

When I woke up in the ICU, I had a huge tube down my throat that I desperately tried to pull out before a nurse appeared, grabbing at my hands to stop me. I couldn't breathe or swallow, and it was the worst feeling. I snatched my hand away from her grasp, trying once again to remove it, but I was more disappointed that I had survived the surgery. The pain was horrific and the worst that I had ever felt or even wanted to ever feel again.

She called out for another nurse, who came to assist, telling me that she would remove the tube, but I had to take a deep breath and exhale slowly as she pulled it out. I choked at that huge thing coming out of my mouth and it made me unable to speak. I insisted she give me some water, but she refused, saying that it was in my best interest not to have any until the surgeon came in to see me. The only thing you could hear on the entire floor was my screaming with pain at what was happening to me. No one had ever taken the time, prior to surgery, to explain that this sadistic torture would be happening to me.

The nurse must have noticed how much pain I was in. She prepared another shot of Demerol and stuck it into my hip. It wasn't long before I could feel the drug starting to work and sleep finally took over, for which I was very grateful. As promised, I was moved from ICU to a semi-private room and put into a bed. All I could do was lie there, staring at the clock on the wall, waiting the four hours until I could get another shot of Demerol.

It was only a day after the surgery when the doctor came in with two nurses, telling me that this was the day that I had to get out of bed. There was no way in hell I was going to do such a thing this soon after surgery, so I yelled at them to get out of my room. They all left, but only for a short time before they returned with two huge orderlies who swooped down and pulled me to an upright sitting position. They held me there for a few minutes until I begged them to let me lie down again, shouting at them to get me more drugs.

Four months had passed with the pain getting only slightly better. The doctors were stumped and told my mom that they were going have to transfer me to a convalescent hospital, where I would be taught to walk again. My mother agreed, and the next day, I was wheeled down to the fracture room, where they slid me onto a thin metal frame meant to prepare me for a body cast, and me lying there buck-naked in the process. The attendant finally came in and proceeded to wrap me in these strips of cold plaster until it covered me from my chest to my hips. Several hours later, when the plaster dried, I was taken back to the same room with another attendant holding this huge circular saw, saying that he would being cutting a hole in the cast around my stomach, so if my stomach expanded after eating, it wouldn't be uncomfortable. This was another horrible experience I couldn't ever have imagined, and I swore I would never have another surgery again. Had I known I would be having fifty plus more surgeries later in my life, I probably would have worked harder to die during this surgery.

When I arrived at the convalescent hospital, I cried out for more Demerol. I was addicted, and I knew it, so I really had to lay heavy on the pain groaning to get more. Instead, they gave me something called

"Dilaudid," a derivative of morphine. It wasn't quite as good as the Demerol, but then again, I knew the drugs weren't going to last forever, so I asked for it as often as I was allowed, and then hoarded what I didn't use then, for later.

I was there for another five months when they told me that I was scheduled to be released. I was having a great time with other patients there and had met a really nice guy, William, who had been in a motorcycle accident and had broken both of his legs. He became a valued friend, whose best friend would break us out at night to go bar hopping. It wasn't easy getting William quickly out into the car without being caught, so I would go first. I would open the back car door as he hobbled out with two full leg casts and his crutches before anyone had noticed. As he got to the car, I shoved him into the back-seat, telling his friend to take-off and then make a hard left turn as quickly as possible. That way the back door would slam shut as we drove off. We, of course, got into big trouble when we returned, but it was a great time that we got away with for another few nights before they announced that my parents were here to take me home. I would really miss William, and I hated the thought of going back my usual hell home. My cast was to be on for another six months before I would go back to the hospital to be fitted for a plastic brace that had to be worn for another entire year.

When the six months came I was placed back on the metal plate again, using the same saw to cut off the cast to make a mold for my brace. It was a thick, clear plastic to keep my spine straight and buckled up in the front like a corset. At the time, I had long, beautiful blond hair that was one of the features men loved most about me, and I wore it atop my head and secured with bobby pins. When they removed the cast, they noticed a dozen or so bobby pins that had fallen into the cast and embedded themselves into the incision. They had to be removed surgically before it got infected. I couldn't believe my luck, and it meant that that they had to give me a local anesthetic to remove them all. They also noticed that their saw had cut deep into my skin while removing the cast, so that now had to be stitched up, meaning another night in the hospital, which I hated. I told my mother not to stay and that I would call her the next day when they released me.

When I called in the morning, mom answered, and I could hear my father in the background furious over something so inconsequential. I told her they weren't releasing me quite yet, and I would call when they did. After thinking about it, I decided that I would take the bus home, giving my dad time to get over whatever drama he had created.

When I arrived back home, just as I had figured, Dad had calmed down and had gone out for a drive. I regretfully relayed the doctor's instructions that I had to stay in bed, but I could only take so much more of that boredom. I kept begging to be let out of my room, saying that I was feeling great and just wanted to visit my friends in the evening, and to see everyone again after so many months.

Finally, I bugged them so much that they agreed to my request, as long as I wasn't out too late. My friends picked me up at the front door that night. I hobbled out to the car with my parents staring at them through the living room window, disgusted at their hairy faces and long hair. I was just so happy to finally have some freedom again, and there wasn't a damned thing they could do about it. I was twenty-one, and an adult now, according to the law.

When my friends announced that we were going downtown to the Gasworks, I got really excited. I was thankful I still had pills leftover from the hospital, but I didn't care how much pain I would be in; I was free.

CHAPTER 26

After a few Bacardi and Cokes, I started feeling a little more at ease, and as I made my way to the bathroom, I nearly fell over this guy who hadn't seen me as he pushed his chair back to get up. He apologized, and it was then that I noticed he was a very attractive man, sitting with his male friends and looking at me as if he was interested. He hesitated somewhat, probably wondering what I must be wearing under my shirt that made my weighted figure stand out of proportion from the rest of my body. I accepted his apology and continued to the bathroom. I found him outside the door when I came out. He took my hand and told me that he wanted to make it up to me by buying me a drink. He invited me to sit with him and his friends; some guy named Dave and his other friend, Tom. In an effort to be cautious, I told him that I would be right back after I went to the bar to retrieve my purse and jacket. I asked the bartender if he had recognized these guys at all. I was looking for some kind of approval that they were safe to sit with. He wasn't much help, saying that he and his friends had been regulars there for the past several weeks and they had never caused any trouble. The bartender went on to explain that he was new and part-time, so he didn't really have too much to say that would help. I decided to take a chance and made my way back to their table.

Jim, whom they called "Bonds" for whatever reason, seemed to be a real gentleman. He took my purse and coat and placed it onto an empty chair while pulling out the chair next to him for me to sit down on. With my experience, I had learned that looks and behavior could be very deceiving, but I was a little inebriated, so my defenses were lower than usual.

Bonds and I had become infatuated with each other throughout the night until the bartender announced, "Last call."

Time had passed too quickly, and it was now 1:00 a.m. I wasn't ready to give Bonds up quite yet, and when he invited me back to his place, I accepted with little hesitation, desperate to finally meet someone who could possibly be the one for me. I never did go home to the suburbs, and we were inseparable over the next few weeks that passed until Bonds asked me to move in with him. Of course, my parents weren't happy that I never did come home after that first night, but I couldn't take living with them anymore or deny myself the possibility of finding a man I could spend the rest of my life with.

The next day, when Mom and Dad were gone, I sneaked home and packed a bag with Bonds waiting out front for me in the car. We left and headed toward our new adventure together as a committed couple, and I couldn't have been happier. It wasn't obvious at the time, but this would become the worst bloody mess I wouldn't think possible, be prepared for, and one that would physically scar me for life.

Bonds smoked what I thought was too much pot and God only knows what else. He lived in a house that he shared with Dave and Tom downtown. I planned to get a job, but I enjoyed playing the doting housewife way too much. It was obvious to Bonds the first night when he took my clothes off that I had been through a grueling surgery after I removed my brace and he examined the fresh scars on my back. The next morning, when I came into the kitchen, the guys were all having breakfast while smiling at me and then announced that my new name was "Myrtle," as in "Myrtle the Turtle." Of course, it was because of the body armor, but I didn't mind. His friends were great, and I was falling in love with Jim.

I always had dinner on the table for everyone when they got home each night. I cleaned and did their laundry during the day, and we all went out together at night, drinking at one of the downtown bars. Things were great until we got home one night, and Dave approached me, telling me that I needed to be careful with Bonds because he had a terrible temper. I thought that I could handle it if what I had seen of him so far was the worst it could get. He yelled a few times when things didn't go his way, but I always consoled him, and he settled down.

The next day, jim announced that we were moving out into our own apartment a few blocks away. I was as surprised as his roommates were, but it was another step closer to what I thought would be a fairytale future together.

It was a small apartment, but one that I could appreciate and love with my man always at my side, up until Jim stopped coming home some nights, and when he did, he was seriously drunk, reeking of women's perfume. When I asked where he had been, he just looked at me with the same dead eyes my father used to have before pushing me aside to go to bed. I became scared, and when going to the bedroom to sleep, I could smell a strong odor about him that people usually gave off right after sex. I got mad and woke him up out of his drunken stupor. As he quickly woke up, this baseball bat seemed to come out of nowhere, and he started swinging it toward me. If I hadn't been out of his swinging range, I would have been dead. I never knew that he kept a baseball bat at arm's length beside him under the bed or even why he felt the need to have one at all.

The next day, I walked over to our old house, where Dave still lived, to try to speak to him about what had happened, and I was thankful to find he was home from work. He just looked at me as if to say, "I told you so." His only advice for me was to get as far away from him as possible at the next opportune moment. Again, I became scared not because of what he told me but what he was leaving out.

Dave was a postal employee and had a gorgeous girlfriend, Shelly, who was a model and striving actress. I always felt intimidated while around her, but she was a down-to-earth person, and I really liked her. She had given me beauty and make-up tips, insisting a particular haircut for me that would accentuate my attractive features, which it did.

The haircut seemed to change the way Jim looked at me, but his carousing with other women still continued, and I wasn't going to stand for it anymore. He came home the next night with news that it was Dave's birthday, and we were going to his party later to celebrate. I too had great news, landing a great job earlier in the day at a hobby manufacturing company as their credit manager. I was to start in the morning and told him that I would go to the party but couldn't stay out too late. He did what he always did and just ignored me, telling me to get dressed for the party.

When we arrived, there were so many people at the house. I spotted Shelly and walked toward her, needing a familiar face to speak to. It grew late very quickly until the clock showed 1:00 a.m. I found Bonds flirting with some whore and told him that we needed to go home, with my new job starting in a few hours.

He was livid, but because I had already told Dave that we had to leave, Jim nearly threw me out the door toward the car in a fit of rage, bitching about the embarrassment I caused him by leaving the party early. I had never seen him so pissed off, and he made me feel every bit of his anger. He threw me into his car and started driving erratically down the street before slamming on the brakes. When I tried to tell him how sorry I was for making him so mad, he threw his right fist out so hard that it hit me across my face, breaking my nose. Blood poured out in every direction as I tried to hide the pain, which only made him madder. He slammed his foot on the brake, throwing me into the windshield, cutting my forehead, and then pulled the car off onto the shoulder to park. He jumped out of the car and came around to my side of the door. He dragged me out of the passenger seat, and threw me to the ground, kicking me as I hid my face while trying to protect myself, but he was huge and so much stronger than I was. He was in such a rage. My plastic brace was protecting me from the damage he wanted to do to my back, and every kick was injuring his feet because of the hard plastic. With one swoop, he threw me up against the car, trying to remove my brace, but I was screaming so loud he was afraid that people would start coming out of their homes and call the police. He opened the car door and threw me back inside with my leg still on the ground, slamming the car door so hard that blood started pouring out from my leg. He threw my leg back into the car, slammed the door and drove off. I was scared he was going to take me somewhere to kill me.

We hadn't driven far when he stopped for a red light, and the car stalled at the intersection. He was out of control by then jumping out of the car, and raising the hood to see why it wouldn't start.

It was just a few minutes when I heard another voice asking what the problem was and if he needed help. I could hear him trying to brush this guy away as soon as possible before he noticed me, and I was afraid of what Jim would do to him if he did. The hood was fully up, but there was a small space between the dashboard and the raised hood that made it possible for me to see that it was a cop who had stopped to help. I tried to show my face within that small space. Our eyes made contact for a quick second before I heard a loud agonizing thump against the car. Seconds later, my car door opened and the cop appeared, noticing all the blood on the inside of the roof, doors, windshield, and me covered in so much blood he had to ask if I was a man or a woman. I saw Jim lying flat on the street handcuffed to the grill of the car, giving me a threatening look to keep my mouth shut.

The beating had caused such horrific pain, but the officer was so calm and very nice to me, trying to get me out of the car. When I told him that I wasn't able to move, he noticed my leg bleeding profusely. Fearful that the artery was damaged and I could lose the leg, he immediately called for an ambulance and the fire/rescue to remove me from the car. He ran to his squad car for a shirt he kept in the backseat that had just been dry cleaned and wrapped it around my leg to stop the bleeding. It had already swollen three times its original size, and he was afraid that I could bleed out by the time I got to the hospital. When the ambulance arrived a few minutes later, they wrapped a tourniquet tightly around my leg and transported me to the hospital with lights and sirens blazing.

The hospital took excellent care of me, set my nose, and fixed my leg, and now after four decades of time that has now passed; the scar on my leg today still reminds me of that terrifying night with Jim. When the officer came back to check on me, I was told that Jim went to jail and would be up on aggravated assault charges. When I told him that we lived together, he could only say that they could keep him for seventy-two hours before his arraignment. That would give me enough time to get my things out of the apartment before he went to court and would probably get released on his "own recognizance."

The hospital released me at six o'clock that morning, giving me only three hours to get back to our apartment, pack, and get to my new job on time by 9:00 a.m. When I told the officer I had no transportation, he recommended that I take the car he had just impounded, and he would waive the fifty-dollar impound fee to give me a head start.

I was grateful and headed back to our apartment to change for work, clean up, and pack my things. It was very difficult with more pain than I wanted to deal with, and I hoped that I wouldn't get fired before I actually started my new job. My right leg was badly damaged, and the doctor's told me that if I hadn't gotten to the hospital when I did, I could have lost the leg, or worse, bled out and died. I struggled through so much pain that the painkillers didn't even make a bit of difference, and together, they made it very difficult to drive. The only other option was to take the officer up on his offer to drive me to work, and explain to my bosses what had happened to me so I wouldn't lose my job. I thought about it for a quick minute before graciously declining; thinking that it wouldn't look very good to my bosses showing up my first day in a police cruiser. I did accomplish what had to be done in the time I had to do it, and headed off to work.

CHAPTER 27

I actually got to work fifteen minutes earlier than my start time. As I tried to casually walk through the front door of the office, hobbling on crutches and wearing several bandages on my face, hands, and leg, I was instantly greeted by the top boss who saw me drive up. He automatically ushered me into his office, telling me to sit down. I hadn't met him before, but he was a very serious dude, and he wasn't looking very friendly toward me. Before I knew it, his brother and their third partner were in the office too, closing the door behind them. They just stared at me, waiting for an explanation. I hadn't really thought of a good one to tell them, so I started to say that I was in a car accident. They just stared as if they knew I was lying, so, I decided to tell them the truth since one of the partners had just returned from examining the car, and it was obvious that the front interior was covered in dried blood, the windshield was cracked where my head made contact, the outside passenger door was literally sprayed in dried blood from my leg, and all of my belongings were quickly thrown into the back seat. Because of the severe damage to my head and leg, the doctor insisted on keeping me in the hospital several days for observation and time for me to heal, but I refused. This job would be a great opportunity for me and I wasn't going to screw it up, so I left against doctor's orders.

Although I was frightened by telling them the truth, I actually felt very at ease, as if for some reason I could trust them. They were very angry as I told them the story, demanding that I not leave anything out. Ben stood up, bellowing that they would not stand for this kind of fucking bullshit with any of their family members. I trembled, thinking that they didn't want any employee of theirs bringing personal crap to the office, yet I was confused with the "family member" reference. I just pretended that I didn't hear that part and settled down just to see what would happen next. It was almost like watching a gangster movie, and I was in it. All of a sudden Ben took the other bosses to a corner of the room, leaving me in my chair, and all I could hear him say was, "Gather the boys." When they returned, they hovered over me as Terry blurted out that they had serious connections, and all I had to do was write Jim's address down on a piece of paper. They would make sure that Jim would never hurt me, or anyone else for that matter, again.

I wasn't used to this kind of treatment, or their solutions to a problem, and it was intimidating to say the least. I was confused with what they were trying to tell me they would do to Jim, but I had a pretty good idea. I hated Jim for what he had done to me over the past few months with the cheatings and the beatings that had gotten out of hand, but I didn't think that he deserved to die for it. Jim was hopefully going to prison for what he had done to me and that seemed good enough for me. Actually, the only person who came to see me in the hospital was Dave when I called to tell him what Jim had done. He came straight to the hospital from the party and he freaked out, standing before me at my bed just before they cleaned me up. He couldn't believe that his friend was so malicious that he would do such a thing. What I also appreciated was that he never once gloated with the "I told you so" I deserved, and should have paid more attention when he was warning me about Jim.

Their office door opened again as if it were an invitation for anyone who wanted to join the party to come in. He was a tall and lanky Indian man, whom I recognized from the previous interview when he hired me. He just stared at me in shock, looking me up and down; noticing the crutches, the broken and bandaged nose, the two black eyes from the broken nose, and the bandage covering my forehead where I received thirteen stitches from hitting the windshield.

I was messed up pretty badly. They told me to take the next few days off, promising that my job would be there when I came back. I didn't have a place to go except for my parent's, and going back there like this was the last thing I would do.

I begged them to let me stay, and at 5:00 p.m. I heard my name called over the PA system, saying that I had a visitor at the front door. As I gimped over, I could see that it was Dave waiting there for me. Everyone else could also see a man waiting for me, and the bosses must have thought it was Jim. I quickly gimped faster into Ben's office while he was on the phone looking pretty pissed off and vengeful. I basically hung up the phone to whoever he was talking to, knowing that Dave wouldn't last 2 minutes when leaving, without a bullet to his brain. I apologized to Ben and told him that Dave had rescued me from Jim on several occasions. Ben headed out to reception with his hand extended to shake Dave's hand, and then pulled him aside for a quick and serious chat that I wasn't privy to.

Dave was amazing. He felt guilty for what had happened to me. When he asked me where I was going to stay, all I could blurt out was that I would sleep in Jim's car until I could find a place of my own. Dave was disturbed by the thought and invited me to live at the new house he had just rented. It was a beautiful home with three bedrooms and Shelly had already agreed. The rent was cheap, and it was very close to work, so I graciously accepted his offer.

Dave loved his job at the post office. He worked short hours in addition to what he called a "small business" on the side, but he never elaborated on what that was. When I asked, he changed the subject and just said that the less I knew the better off I would be. I had no idea what he was talking about, but it was a great home, and he was a good friend, so I never pushed for details.

CHAPTER 28

We lived very comfortably for a few weeks while I completely healed. Dave was always there at my side helping me with whatever I needed.

Eventually, I had to give Jim's car back, but this new place with Dave was far and I really needed a car to get to work. On the last day of having the car, Terry came up to me and invited me into his office for a conversation. I was doing really well as their credit manager, so the thought of me being fired had never crossed my mind. Somehow, he knew of my transportation problem and told me that he had connections with a car dealership, and that he would be happy to co-sign a car loan for me. I jumped at the opportunity, and after work, he drove me to the dealership. Within minutes, his friend had given me a great price and an easy payment plan I could afford, and I drove off the lot with my new Pacer. Things were finally coming together for me. I was living at Dave's, and I was now independent; I owned my own vehicle, had a great job, and had made new friends with power should I have any further problems with Jim. Things were finally looking up in my life, and I was grateful for everything.

A few more weeks passed, and I was becoming quite popular with the other employees and sales staff, and during in-house company events, Jack from the warehouse would bring in some of his great Jamaican weed for everyone to smoke, including the bosses and clients. I even had my own little stash of Bailey's liqueur that I loved and kept in the toilet tank just outside of my office. It was great. The bosses had given me expense accounts to wine-and-dine my delinquent clients; basically to get them drunk until they gave me a check for the money they owed. I was a natural at the job and was always appreciated and praised for my good work.

Most of my delinquent clients resented me because, if necessary, I would remove all of our stock from their stores before they declared bankruptcy. I didn't really like what I had to do, but I got paid well to travel all over Ontario, collecting money and doing a job that made me look good at work.

One night, I was covering several small towns in eastern Ontario visiting my delinquent accounts, trying to get paid, or threatening to foreclose on their inventory. It was late, maybe midnight, when I finished and stopped off at a bar to have a couple of white Russians before heading home. It was 1:00 a.m. when I finally got into my car, and I was hitting pretty high speeds, trying to make good time. All of a sudden the car's electronics cut out, and I lost control of my car. Thankfully, I wasn't wearing a seat belt when my car headed toward a speed limit sign at the side of the highway where I crashed and came to a grinding stop. Seconds before impact, I flatten myself down onto the passenger seat, avoiding the sign as it smashed through the windshield and took the backrest of my seat completely off where my head would have been. There was flying glass and stuffing from the seat everywhere, which was totally destroyed. Once again, I found myself covered in blood from head to toe. I managed to crawl out of the car and fell into a ditch. I straightened myself up and looked at the carnage I had escaped from and couldn't believe it. It was amazing that I survived.

Within seconds I could see an eighteen-wheeler in the distance coming toward me and I stuck my thumb out. I had no idea where to go, or what my injuries were, but I was outside the city limits and could only think of one person to go to: Jack from the warehouse. We were having a bit of a casual relationship a few times a month, so I knew where he lived, and we were already pretty close to his place. The truck driver was very concerned with the way I looked and insisted on an ambulance, but I talked him into just driving me to Jack's place.

When I knocked at 2:00 a.m., it took a few minutes for him to come to the door. When he opened it, he freaked out at so much blood covering me. He thanked the truck driver for bringing me and was told the location of my car. Jack cleaned me up the best he could, and I passed out in his bed, making him promise not to tell my boss what had happened or to mention that I had two drinks before coming home. After all, I was convinced that the alcohol was the reason I survived such a devastating crash.

In the morning shortly after Jack had gone to work, there was a knock at the front door, and my boss appeared in front of me. I couldn't believe that Jack had sold me out like that.

My boss, Damien, was very sympathetic about what had happened as he pushed by me into Jack's house. He sat on the sofa and motioned me to sit down and tell him what had happened. Of course, I wasn't going to tell him that I was drinking, while driving home from one of the client's businesses he sent me to, so I just stayed with the facts, which were fuzzy at best from the shock. He told me to get dressed, and we would go together to find my car. As we drove east, we both noticed my car on the opposite side of the highway with a cop looking it over with extreme interest. Damien told me not to say anything and that he would do all the talking. He got out of the car and approached the cop, who asked who we were and told Damien that this was one of the most horrific accidents he had seen since becoming a cop. He continued to say that a rescue team had been searching for the body for hours because no one could have possibly survived. It was then that my boss told him I was the driver sitting in his car.

The cop was totally shocked, wondering how the hell I had survived after viewing the back-rest of my seat, which was totally demolished, the totally blown-out windshield, and all the blood on the interior of the car. The hood was up, and I couldn't quite hear what they were saying, but the cop was pointing to something seriously wrong, and explaining it to Damien in detail. When they came over and opened my car door, I was trembling, listening to the cop tell my boss that someone had planted a "sand bomb" in my car. He asked where I had been the previous night and what I had done to make someone so pissed off that they would do this to me. I still had the six checks in my purse from the collections that I did, and as I pulled them out of my wallet, I told the cop that I was a credit manager and collector for the company.

Damien took control of the conversation again, curiously asking what a sand bomb was. The cop described it as a very simple compressed bomb made of sand that when placed under the hood in a particular position, and when the car reached a certain set speed, it would trigger the bomb, disengaging the car's electronics. I didn't understand it but Damien looked satisfied with the explanation. I never did find out which client tried to kill me that night. For me, this was a catastrophic close-call, and I was thankful it was over, and I survived. Actually this was only a minor hiccup compared to the next sequence of events I managed to find myself in.

Damien insisted on taking me to the hospital to get checked out, which took hours in the emergency room. The blood on my head continued slowly leaking down my face, and required stitches. The CT-scan showed a slight concussion but I refused to stay overnight for observation, and just told Damien it was never offered. I just wanted to go back to Jack's place, take the pain pills they gave me, and sleep until the morning before going back to work. Of course, Damien gave me hell for that too, as did the bosses when I showed up for work looking like I had just been through a leaf-grinder.

I started to recall everything I could that led up to the explosion. I had visited several clients that night to collect money, and they were still in my purse. I handed all of them to Damien as he studied them with intense consideration. I suggested that I deposit the checks immediately, and if one of them bounced, that would be a good indication of the person who planted the bomb. My opinion was that the client would have given me their check knowing that I wouldn't survive the crash, and, therefore, his check would have probably been destroyed in the aftermath of the accident. We had six suspects who could have done this terrible thing, but I was well liked and respected by most of them for just doing my job, and I couldn't think of one who would go so far as to try to kill me.

I was gone by the time Jack returned from work. He was engaged to another woman, whom I did not want to meet. I would have to explain the circumstances of my being there with her fiancé, so Dave picked me up after work at the house and took me home, unable to understand after viewing the pictures I showed him of the car, how I could have possibly survived.

Once we got home, Dave suggested that I indulge in a sample of what he called his "anti-stress reliever" for extreme situations like this, and as he poured the white powder onto the table, he handed me a rolled-up $100 bill. Without hesitation, I quickly took the bill and snorted the drug he put in front of me.

I never realized at the time that Dave was into that kind of stuff but welcomed it with open arms. Shelly had already left for the night, so Dave and I sat there until the wee hours of the morning, talking about everything that came to mind, including Jim and Shelly. We were bonding like we were such close friends and it felt great. I never went to sleep that night, but in the morning, I felt as though I could conquer the world, so I showered and dressed for work against Dave's suggestion to stay home for another day.

It was obvious that Dave had something important on his mind, so he proceeded to tell me that aside from his post office job, he had somehow gotten himself involved with another certain business that he needed to discuss with me, in complete confidence. It was obvious that he was holding back on the particular details, but he went on to say that this business included drugs, and required my total discretion at all times with any transactions he did within the house. For both of our health and safety sake, we had to keep a very low profile so as not to cause any attention to him, or his employers. I told him that he was the only real friend I had, that I didn't care about any side business he might have, and would never betray his trust.

When I got to work the next week, there was an announcement from the receptionist that a client was there to see me, and as I walked to the door, I saw that it was a client from Montreal, who owed us a lot of money. I motioned for him to come to my office, and he sat across from me at my desk. It was getting close to noon, so I invited him out for lunch just up the street from the office. It was my job to get him to pay what he owed, and I knew I could get the money from him. We started off lunch with a couple carafes of wine, a light meal, and then several Spanish coffees that I loved to seal the deal with.

When my phone rang, I was hesitant to answer it. With his check-book now in hand, Serge told me to go ahead with the call. It was my secretary calling to tell me that I needed to get back to the office as soon as possible. I hadn't gotten Serge's check yet so I probed her for more information until she finally told me that my father had been taken to the hospital after having a major stroke. I knew I was drunk beyond driving, but the news mentally sobered me up. Serge offered to drive me, but I jumped up as if I hadn't heard him, paid the bill, and nearly ran back to the office to get my car and head to the hospital.

Serge and I had been having a casual relationship since I started working at the office and would meet up every time he was in town. He was gorgeous and in the midst of a divorce, but none of that mattered right then. I wasn't sure whether I needed to go to the hospital to see the bastard who ruined my life because he was my father, or if I just wanted to make sure that he would be dead by the time I got there.

It had started to rain very heavily when I got into

my car. It would take at least an hour on the highway before I could get across town to the hospital, and I didn't want him to die before I got there. This could be my last chance to give him a piece of my mind whether he was conscious or not.

It was early fall and the roads were slippery from the rain, making it treacherous to drive, and the alcohol wasn't helping either, but I was determined to get there as soon as I could. The off-ramp to the hospital from the 401 was finally coming up, and as I headed onto it, the car in front of me slammed on the brakes, causing me to rear-end their car. As we both got out, I could see a hefty black woman exiting and turning on me with fury as if it was my fault. Memories of my father's prejudice against black people crept into my mind as I fought hard to ignore it, but in the moment, so many obscenities spewed out of my mouth uncontrollably and against my better judgment. She came at me like a bat out of hell, saying that she had called the police and they would be there shortly. I needed to go to the hospital to unleash my resentment before it was too late. Unfortunately, I had no choice now to do that. There was no doubt in my mind with my behavior and awkwardness that the cops would give me a breathalyzer test, and I would fail.

The cops showed up within minutes, and I tried desperately to appear sober, but the cop wasn't fooled.

He handcuffed me, covering his nose and mouth from the smell of all the alcohol on my breath, and ushered me into the backseat of his cruiser. I wasn't going to make it to the hospital anytime soon, so I continued to insist that the woman I hit was in the wrong for stopping so abruptly on the ramp, trying to convince him that she had done it purposely, with her extreme prejudice against white people.

At the station, I was able to make a phone call, so I called Dave to come and get me out of there as soon as he was free. It seemed like forever being in the police station behind bars. I was told to empty my purse out onto the table in front of me while three officers supervised me. I had no drugs or alcohol in the car so that was to my advantage. I was ushered into a cell with the worst type of women you could imagine. I tried desperately, to tell the cops that it wasn't my fault, but they had produced a breathalyzer at the scene, which I failed with a very high blood-alcohol level. They said for my weight, they were amazed that I could even walk, let alone drive.

Finally, I was called toward the bars of my cage and was told that I would be staying the night until the judge saw me the next morning at 10:00 a.m., for my arraignment. It didn't take much for me to fall asleep on the iron cots I was forced to lie upon. The hangover in the morning was horrific, but I noticed Dave was in the courtroom when my name was called. Dave had been my best friend up until then. We had shared so many secrets, and I was very fortunate to know that he was there for me when I needed him, even when making so many stupid mistakes. I owed Dave so much for everything he did for me, at least until it graduated from bad to shocking in a matter of hours.

CHAPTER 29

The judge released me, being my first offense, and thankfully, Dave was there to take me home after I picked up the contents of my purse from the table. As I was putting everything back into my purse, I noticed the table beside me had all of the police notebooks that were handed in from the day before when I was arrested. Those books contained everything the cops needed for their arrests: time, weather, arresting officer, and the most miniscule details to make their cases in court. That's when I noticed the name of the cop who arrested me on the top of the book pile, so I took the book, thinking that if he didn't have his notes for court, I could somehow escape the inevitable conviction.

As I picked up the book, I noticed no one had actually paid any attention to me putting it into my purse. An officer then came up to me, and I started to tremble, thinking I had been caught, but he was only there to tell me that Dave had arrived to pick me up. First, they said that they needed to speak to him before releasing me, and I had no idea as to why. They escorted both Dave and me into an interview room where we sat waiting for almost an hour before a detective appeared with a concerned look on his face.

I was totally embarrassed when the detective mentioned to Dave that I was "slamming" drugs. They had strip searched me when I got arrested and noticed the fresh marks on my arms. During the hour we waited, the cops had done a background check on Dave, finding him to be an upstanding postal employee with no criminal record, and that made a big difference when releasing me into his supervision.

Dave didn't have a clue that I was pilfering from his stash of cocaine, and the idea of my using a needle for the cocaine totally caught him off guard. Of course, he denied any knowledge of it and just stared at me with disgust. He promised the detective he would keep an eye on me, and we left the station in total silence. The ride home was very quiet, and I wasn't going to break the ice by starting any conversation that would lead to the drugs I was taking from him.

When we got home, Dave ordered me over to the sofa. He paced back and forth with a scowl, reminding me that because of his post office position, the Italian Mafia had forced him to work for them as one of their major drug dealers. He made it clear that these people were very dangerous and that he had to have trust in me not to draw attention to him or to them, whatsoever, in any way, if we both wanted to live.

Again, I swore that I would never do anything to hurt Dave with all he had done for me, so I promised to do better, and I meant it. As Dave stood up satisfied that I understood the situation, I calmly admitted that I may have taken the cop's notebook from the table at the station, explaining why.

I had never seen Dave so pissed off at what I had done. He started flailing his arms, yelling at how stupid I was and that I didn't understand the serious repercussions this would have on us both if the cops came to the house looking for it.

He went on saying that he had fifty kilos of pot, three kilos of cocaine, and 2,500 MDA pills being delivered to the house later in the day that he had to accept and distribute for the Mafia. I could see him searching for words. He told me to take a quick shower and that we would go back to the station to return the book before they came looking for it. While I was in the shower, he ordered a pizza that would be there within thirty minutes. I did stop at my bedroom first to snort some leftover cocaine I secretively stashed before the arrest, and I needed it desperately after what had happened, especially without Dave knowing what I was doing.

While I was in the bathroom, Dave was on the sofa in the living room, counting out more money than I would ever see in my lifetime to pay for his drug shipment. He had a special hiding spot in the basement that the Mafia had built for the drugs to avoid detection, and it was specifically lined with something so that the K9 unit dogs would be thrown off the scent. Unfortunately, the previous drugs still left in the basement were pulled out to allow for the new drugs to be placed in first, and the older stash was a significant amount just laying on the floor in open view.

Right behind the sofa that Dave was on, was a ten-foot bay window without drapes, showing everything we did in the house and totally visible from the street. I had asked him several times to cover it for privacy, but he never got around to doing it, and that was a huge mistake on his part.

The shower was running, so I couldn't hear the commotion going on downstairs. Just as I was getting in the shower, I heard a heavy knock on the bathroom door with a voice I didn't recognize. I told them I was naked and to wait a minute. The man at the door identified himself as a police officer, and told me if I didn't open the door immediately, they would break it down. I freaked out but managed to wrap a towel around me.

The cop standing before me had his gun drawn. He commanded me to get dressed, and told me that we were both under arrested as the handcuffs were slapped onto us both. We were being arrested for narcotics trafficking. Again, I found myself in another worst possible situation. The only exception this time was that this arrest could easily send me to prison for more than fifteen years or get me killed by these perilous Mafia people, if what Dave had just told me was true. At the police station, they ushered us into separate interrogation rooms with Dave looking as if he could kill me for what I had done to him and what the Mafia would do to us both when they found out what I had done.

In the car on the way to the station, Dave leaned over and whispered that there was a very good chance I would have to own up to the drug possession and trafficking charges, myself. He knew that once the cops searched the entire house, they would find all of the drugs leftover from the last shipment in the basement. He made sure that I understood that these people he worked for would kill me and my family if I didn't do it, and Dave was way too valuable to lose with his position at the post office. My jaw dropped at the thought. I knew nothing about drugs except for doing them periodically to forget what I could about my appalling childhood.

I couldn't move and was still in shock, but somehow, my head nodded in agreement as I thought of my mother and the pain she would suffer with me going to prison, or being a victim of a brutal mob murder. We were soon both behind the bars that separated us in the police jail cells before our arraignment by the judge later that day. Fortunately, we both got released with the promise to return to court a few weeks later. I wasn't sure how I was going to tell my boss about this crap, so I took a sick day to give my mind time to work out what I knew was a hopeless situation.

I had already lost my license and my car when my court case came up for the DUI case several days earlier. All of my bosses came to court with me and had hired me a lawyer to fight the case with the circumstances of my father dying in the hospital. It was a surprise and relief when they told me they would pay the legal costs for me because of my value, my age, and the fact that I didn't have that kind of money. I was very grateful, but when they took away my license and car, I wasn't sure how I was going to get to work. I could learn to take the bus and calculate the two-hour bus ride to work each way when Dave couldn't drive me or my boss stopped sending his limo for me. I was pretty sure that Dave was going to evict me from the house and alienate me prior to our court date, but it never happened. The Mafia had a different approach that I wasn't prepared for, and I was terrified.

Standing before the judge, I found out it was actually a condition of our release and in both of our best interests that Dave and I did not live together, and we would be tried separately. Dave looked scared with the judgment but at the same time he was relieved knowing I was going to take the rap for the drugs. At least with my living at the house, he could keep an eye on me to make sure I went to court.

As the days passed at work, I avoided Damien like the plague. He was laying on so much charm and making so many sexual advances toward me that I was very uncomfortable going into his back office for supplies. He had done so much for me over the past several months, and I guess that he thought I owed him at least a quickie or two for his trouble. At the same time, I felt that if I pushed him away too many times, he might turn the owners against me as well. I casually refused his advances just the same, not caring what happened to me. After all, I was going to prison for a very long time in just a few short weeks.

The Jamaican pot Jack brought in daily was helpful as was the rum I kept with the Baileys in the bathroom tank, but it just didn't seem to be enough. I hadn't told anyone about the upcoming court case, so I was on my own trying to figure it out. I was scared of my own shadow and more so when I went home each night while Dave sat staring at me as if he wanted to say something, trying to determine exactly what I would say when we went to court. I never did comply with the judge's order to vacate the house, and no one ever came to check that I did. In the back of my mind, I knew these Mafia people wouldn't permit it anyway, proven by the car parked outside our house twenty-four/seven, and the car that was following me everywhere I went. If I met someone I knew on the street and stopped to say hi, shortly thereafter, two huge intimidating men would accidently bump into me, forcing me to acknowledge their presence. They would also hold their jackets open, revealing the guns they had sticking out of their pants. My life was not my own anymore, and again, I was terrified with what would happen to me.

CHAPTER 30

Our court case was only a few days away, and the goons who kept parked out front and periodically came into the house were scary, to say the least. The obvious bulge showed the blunt end of their guns, making it clear and obvious that I could be killed at a moment's notice. Whenever they tried to talk to me alone, Dave would assure them that they had nothing to worry about, that we constantly talked about the upcoming case, and there was no doubt in his mind that I would do what they wanted of me in court.

It seemed as though the next few days flew by way too quickly with Dave watching my every move. Whenever he got up to go to the bathroom, I would steal some of the cocaine he always seemed to have in front of him. It made me courageous and opened up thoughts inside my head that made me think beyond what I normally could do. I had an uncanny ability to survive, and somehow, I knew I would get through this too. I just wasn't sure how I would do it. Every night was sleepless with my mind working overtime trying to find a solution, and it was taking its toll on me. I was exhausted and looked twenty-years older than I was from the extreme stress.

I had grown up constantly stressed out, whether I was awake or asleep, always on guard for anyone lurking in the shadows or around every corner ready to attack me. With Dave always there for me, my guard was slightly lower, but with the Mafia thugs always parked in front of our house, I never felt completely safe. In the morning, our court case would be heard, and I still didn't have an antidote for my situation. I remembered Dave's serious speech the night before reminding me of my duty to do this right with no mistakes and what would happen to me and my family if I didn't comply. I couldn't sleep for worrying about what I would say while at the same time, wondering how long I would last if I denied possession of the drugs. After all, I was looking at a minimum fifteen year prison sentence if convicted or a bullet to my brain. Just the thought terrified me, and I knew that my life would be over either way.

We drove together to the courthouse, and I sat there beside myself, trembling with the consequences that were minutes away. When the clerk called out my case number, I rose as requested and sat in the witness box beside the judge, raising my hand and swearing to tell the truth, so help me God. I knew that even God couldn't help me this time.

I was twenty-one years old, and right off the bat, I lied when I was asked my age, saying I was seventeen, just like the Mafia instructed me to do. The judge just kept staring at me when suddenly the courtroom doors opened, and three huge frightening men entered and sat in the last row of the gallery.

After they sat down, the judge turned to me and rudely interrupted the crown attorney who was questioning me. He asked me how many kilos were in a pound. Since I wasn't a drug dealer or a metric person by any means, I looked him straight in the eyes, still trembling, but remembering my mother being torture to death if I didn't cooperate. I replied in a confident tone that ten kilos were equivalent to a pound, and that the drugs were mine, and I was so sorry for what I had done, begging him for mercy. The next question he asked was exactly how many drugs were confiscated from my basement at the time of my arrest. That completely caught me off-guard, and I had absolutely no idea whatsoever. I was never privy to that kind of information, nor was I prepped by the Mafia with how to answer it. There were so many drugs in the basement, so I thought it would be reasonable to say that there was five-hundred and seventy-five kilos that were confiscated.

It took only a few seconds for the judge to call a

thirty-minute recess, claiming a family emergency. He directed the bailiff to clear the courtroom, and once that was done, he ordered the bailiff to escort me to his chambers. As the bailiff and I arrived, the judge just stared at me silently behind his desk and ordered the bailiff to leave and for me to sit. When he finally spoke, he asked me if I had recognized the men who had just walked through the courtroom doors. I didn't have a clue, so I just shook my head in denial. The judge continued on to tell me that they were hit-men for the Mafia, and he guessed that I was being set up to take responsibility for the drugs. Undoubtedly, and failing that, I wouldn't last two minutes after leaving the courthouse if I wasn't convicted. I started to cry hysterically, blurting out the entire truth about what had happened to me. He pushed his hand up to stop me and sat silently for a few minutes before telling me that I was in more trouble than I could possibly imagine. He hesitated for another moment as if contemplating his next move and then ordered me to stand. His driver quickly appeared from a hidden door at the back of his office. He looked right past me as if I weren't there, telling his driver to take me home, help me pack my things quickly, and drive me to the train station where I would pick a destination and never come back to Toronto ever again.

"Do you want to live, young lady?" he asked.

"Yes, sir," I replied, still shaking.

"Have you learned anything from this experience?" he shouted, scaring me more.

"Yes I have, sir!"

"You have twenty-four minutes before court convenes again, at which time I will order the court to recess until tomorrow morning at nine o'clock for your case to be heard." "That should give you enough time to disappear safely, so make the most of it!" "I will go back into the courtroom and make the judgment that you will be held over in jail until then, and give specific instructions to the jail captain to confirm, should anyone inquire." "That will buy you more time and give you twenty-three hours from now to lose yourself somewhere before court convenes." "Get the hell out of here *now!*" he screamed, making sure that I totally understood that he was saving my life and to take him seriously.

Before any of this could register properly in my brain, the driver pulled me out the door as fast as we could run. He also assured me that there would be a car posted outside my parents' home so as not to have anything happen to them. I was relieved to hear that, telling the driver that these people threatened to torture my family to death if I didn't comply. The driver looked at me through the rearview mirror and told me how lucky I was to get his boss as my judge. He was very anti-Mafia and knew that he was saving my life. The rest was up to me, and I wasn't going to let either of us down.

I had exactly eleven minutes from the time we arrived home to get my things packed and head for the train station. First, we would do a drive-by along my street to make sure that no one had followed us, or was waiting for us when we got there. From the backseat, I could see the driver's gun holstered at his side. When looking a little harder at his right leg on the pedal, I noticed a second gun holstered at his ankle. I was terrified but felt very safe with whomever this driver actually was.

I ran into the house and just threw everything I could find into a suitcase. I ran out to the car when I heard a bang that sounded like gunfire. The driver quickly ushered me into the car with his gun drawn, and we escaped without further fire. He drove erratically for several blocks in the opposite direction of the train station just to be sure that we weren't being followed. The tears were flowing down my face, and I cried hysterically as we drove. He assured me that the gun was just a precaution and that an old car driving by had backfired. I wasn't sure if I believed him, but it settled me down a bit just the same.

As we got to the train station, he told me to stay in the car while he went into the office to pay for my ticket. We decided on Montreal. There had been a lot of controversy in the news about Quebec wanting to separate, and everyone knew I didn't speak French, so it seemed like the perfect place to live. I couldn't believe that the judge paid for my ticket. He must have really despised the Mafia, and I'm sure there were some very grueling stories behind why he would want to help me. When I asked the driver about it, he replied, "They murdered his wife and daughter!"

After returning from the ticket counter, my driver pulled out and drove through the parking lot, observing anyone who might have followed us. Once it was safe to continue, he got me out of the car and took my bag as the train was pulling into the station. He advised me to never talk about this to anyone once I got to Montreal, and then handed me an envelope filled with several bills of large denominations that would help me get started in a city I knew nothing about. What I did know about Quebec was while they were trying to separate, they weren't too friendly or receptive to anyone outside their province, and especially to those who didn't speak their language. The driver waited outside the train below my window, with his hand conveniently placed at his waist near his gun and ready for action. As the train pulled out of the station thirty minutes later, I could still see the driver staring diligently at me, from the station, as I disappeared from his sight.

It was a long ride until we arrived at the Montreal

station. I had to call Damien to tell him that I had to leave Toronto for personal reasons, and wouldn't be coming to work anymore. When he asked where I was, I made him promise not to tell anyone I was there that he couldn't trust, and said I would explain later. He wouldn't accept that explanation, and I trusted him with my life, so I told him that it was a life-and-death situation, and if any of this got out, my family and I would be killed. I had already said too much, but it still wasn't good enough for him. I told him that I had stumbled innocently onto criminal activity initiated by the Italian Mafia. That stopped him short of asking more questions, mostly because of his bosses' involvement in their own Mafia activities, and he guaranteed me he would keep his mouth shut. No matter what, I trusted Damien, maybe because of the molestation and the love he pronounced for me every day at work, which I could always hold over him if necessary. He told me that it was extremely important to call him back later in the day, and made me promise. When I did, I was surprised to hear that they had just bought over a huge hobby distribution center in Montreal. He asked me if I would be interested in being their credit manager, mainly to be their eyes and ears for them in Toronto with what was happening, and to submit a daily report with anything serious they should be aware of. I jumped at the opportunity, and I couldn't believe my luck.

He gave me the address of the company and my new boss's name, telling me not to trust anyone there or mention anything to anyone about my situation or our earlier conversation. I agreed, hung up the phone, and started making my way across town to the office.

CHAPTER 31

When I entered the building, no one would speak English to me except for Greg, the boss. As I introduced myself, he pulled me into his office and sat me down after just hanging up with Damien, not looking very happy about the conversation, or me for that matter.

"So," he said as he looked at me suspiciously, "You must have some pretty good pull at head office for them to make you our new credit manager without consulting me first." I gulped, hoping that he wouldn't notice and then stood up, standing over him in his chair, and told him that I would get results whether he liked it or not. He sneered, looking back at me, wondering what the hell I could do that he couldn't after the company takeover. I had to smile in response with him not knowing a damned thing about me or my past. This was a challenge I would take on with full force, thinking at the same time that this was nothing compared to what I had just gone through and I could do it with my eyes closed. At least it was what I thought, until it got real bad, real fast.

I cut to the chase and told him to show me the financials of the company and the outstanding receivables. The figures showed a deficit of $800,000 outstanding from just the past four years. When I asked where my office was, he just looked at me and said that I could take a corner of his office until I proved myself, probably so he could keep an eye on me. I could see that he trusted the Toronto office as much as they trusted him. I gave him the impression that if there was something to expose, I would be the one to do it. I told him that this accommodation would be fine for a couple of days only, but by the first of the week, I needed a private working space if I was going to produce the results expected of me, and if that wasn't done, I would be calling head office. He was hesitant, before he reluctantly accepted my request.

My suitcase sat beside me in his office as he looked questioningly at it. I noticed his stare and told him that I had just gotten off the train and asked if he knew of any apartments close to the office in a good area. I added that I was also promised a car to drive in the deal. It was a lie, but I knew I had the upper hand and it had to be done quickly before the paperwork of my driving suspension went through and possibly reached Quebec.

I could tell that he liked my aggressive behavior. He got out of his chair and motioned me to follow him out the door. As we walked out, I asked where we were going, and he just looked at me as if I was wasting his time. We got into his car and drove a few streets over to an apartment building his wife used to own before she passed away from cancer not long before, and I felt bad for his loss.

He handed me the keys to the apartment, and walking in, I could tell that it was just a studio apartment on the second floor of a low-rise building. It was convenient, satisfactory, very affordable, and I took it right there on the spot. He walked out, and I followed him back to the car asking where we were going next. He told me we had to discuss my salary and benefits at the corner bar.

I told him that we needed make a quick stop first at the DMV so I could take my written driver's test as soon as possible and questions were not an option. He quickly told me that there were differences in the Ontario test versus the Quebec test, so trusting him, I asked what they were and then threatened him that if he lied to me he would be out of a job. Right then, he realized just how much pull I had with Toronto, and I loved the power.

The test went well, and upon passing it, we went directly to the bar. Greg ordered a Bacardi and Coke while I ordered a white Russian. He just stared at me and then called me a "pussy" for the drink I ordered. Before the waitress left with our order, I added a double shot of Scotch and a hamburger to soak up the alcohol. I had never tasted Scotch before, but I'd be damned if anyone would call me a "pussy" after what I just went through the past few months in Toronto.

It was before noon and a little early for me to start drinking, but I wasn't going to be intimidated by his behavior. He was testing me with everything he said and did, but I kept the drinks coming until I noticed how drunk he was getting when I was as sober as a "pussy."

I told him if I was going to live up to my reputation and expectations, I needed a good salary, clothing, and client allowance, and that the company would be paying for my car and gas expenditures. Greg never flinched at the demands, which made me think that I was too quick to ask, and I could have gotten a lot more out of him if I had had more time to consider it. He just nodded and told me that I had better be good at my job and he would give me an answer in the morning once he ran it by Damien in Toronto. I knew Damien would never agree to my demands, but then he really had no choice with his obsession over me and what I could do to him if he didn't agree. I needed the car to call on delinquent clients, a clothing allowance to buy some decent fashionable clothes, and a salary that wouldn't leave me broke living in this expensive city.

Greg made the proposal the next morning while I was out buying furniture and a turntable to learn French. He was impressed with the little time it took to get everything done, and as I looked at my watch, I told him that I was leaving for the day to wait for my furniture to be delivered.

He just nodded and put his head back down into the stack of paperwork on his desk. After the delivery, I made my way downtown to buy clothes, and after a few hours, I was happy with my purchases. Montreal was known for their stylish fashions, and I looked great.

I walked into the office the next morning and asked to meet the rest of the staff. I remembered Damien telling me that there were very crooked people there and the company was losing a lot of money daily. I was going to figure out one way or another who they were, with or without Greg's help. I wasn't even sure whether he was also part of the conspiracy. Most of the office staff was receptive to me so as not to lose their jobs, but in the warehouse, the men just stared at me, making sexist comments and swearing under their breath with French words that I didn't understand. Resentment was written all over their faces with the fact that I was from Ontario.

I'm sure they were wondering just how much damage I could do working there.

Greg told me that my first assignment was to collect a $10,000 debt by a hobby owner who lived just outside the city, and then threatened that returning empty-handed was not an option. As I drove down the highway trying to figure out how the hell to get there, I noticed that for miles there was nothing but dead, isolated highways without a person, car, or house in sight. I quickly understood why this guy wasn't making any money but also questioned why Greg would authorize shipments to such a desolate location.

When I finally did find his shop, I parked to the side of the store and walked up to the front door. It was as if he was expecting me, and as he opened the door, I couldn't believe how enormous this man was hovering over me with the most intimidating face. He led me into the store and looked me straight in the eye, asking if Greg had told me anything about him. I told him he hadn't as he walked over to a magazine rack, smiling proudly as he pulled out a magazine and rifled through it.

When he finished, he took the magazine and stuffed it into his pants, inviting me outside to his Cadillac. I was confused watching as he opened the trunk. It was a little weird, but I'd seen worse, so I went along with it. Again, he asked me if Greg had told me anything about him, but I just shook my head with a look that said it was of no importance, and that he was starting to bore me. As I walked closer to his car, I could see the cache of military guns, hand grenades, packages of Military-grade C-4 explosives, and what looked to be a rocket launcher I saw once on television.

I was scared, but if I had learned anything from my recent experience, it was to show no fear, and if he wanted me dead, he could have done it already. I gulped, hoping he hadn't noticed the fear I was hiding on my face and then looked him straight in the eye, casually admitting that his toys were impressive and reminded him I was there to pick up the money he owed us, and I wasn't leaving without a check.

He bellowed out this daunting laugh while still staring me down with a threatening glare. It scared the crap out of me only because it caught me off guard, and as he looked for some kind of fear in me, I wasn't about to give him the satisfaction, and surprisingly I laughed right back at him. When he didn't get what he wanted, his demeanor changed and he told me that he could blow me up right then and there, and no one would ever find my body. I just sneered at him, thinking that Greg had somehow set me up for this guy to frighten me off. Then he pulled out the magazine he hid in his pants and showed me what he thought would have a greater effect on me. I took the magazine from him with two fingers as if I would catch some kind of disease with it coming out of his pants and saw the cover titled *"Mercenary Magazine."* I was having second thoughts at that point but knew he couldn't have had it printed up so quickly before I arrived. The page he had dog-eared was his own advertisement, listing him as a mercenary, specialized in killing politician's and VIP's for $75,000 cash, no questions asked, with proof of death. I hoped my body language wouldn't give me away when I casually looked up to him, and said, "Cool, Dave. Where's my fucking money?"

"Oh my God," I thought to myself, *"What the hell did Greg get me into?"* Again, I thought I was dead, but I just steadied myself, almost cringing at the thought of never getting out of there alive. From out of nowhere, I heard myself asking him again if he was going to pay me the money or not. I was surprised hearing the words come out of my mouth while still trying to portray the tough bitch he wasn't expecting. Thoughts poured through my mind about the Mafia incident, my childhood survival, and the guy Roger nearly killed. They say that your life flashes through your mind when you're about to die, but I was just getting pissed off at this asshole trying to intimidate me, and I wanted to make sure that it showed on my face.

Again, he freaked me out by spinning himself

around quickly, now with his back toward me, removing something else from the pocket of his pants. I feared that it could be a gun and braced myself for a bullet to my head, still trying to keep myself strong. Instead, he let off another bout of gross laughter that echoed through the dead highways, and several birds shot out from the trees. I had felt this kind of terror before, but now I was up against another damned assassin, standing right in front of me, and in the middle of nowhere. He was a pro, and I knew he could kill me at any time, in any place, for any reason, and there was nowhere for me to run or even hide. He quickly spun around once again, where I couldn't see what was in his hands. I was panicking but still staring into his face as calmly as I could. He turned me around until I could feel his hands pressing heavily on my back. There was total silence until he turned me back again to face him, this time with a check in his hand that he had written on my back for $6,000. He warned me in such an intimidating voice that the next time Greg sent out some little bad-assed bitch to do his dirty work for him that he wasn't going to be so generous and that person would suffer the consequences on Greg's behalf. He smiled and slapped me on the back so hard I nearly fell over, but I grabbed the check from him and headed to my car.

I admit my legs were controlling my speed in getting there as quickly as I could, while still worried about his car trunk, which was still open and that rocket launcher he could use at any time while I drove off. When I saw him heading back into the store, I noticed his keys were still in the trunk lock. After driving past the front of the store, Dave must have gone into the back room, so I stopped, sneaked out of the car, and very quickly removed the keys. Taking no chances, I threw them into the trunk, slamming it shut, and jumped back into my car before he noticed what I had done. The adrenaline made me shake while I was racing off, staring at him in the rearview mirror, watching him run to his car, proving to him that I wasn't as stupid as he thought. I knew he couldn't catch me without the keys, but just the same, I sped out of there like I was on fire in case he had another set of keys close by. He just stared at me as I quickly drove off, and I could hear his last words, "You fucking bitch!" Then surprisingly, he waved good-bye with such a demonic look, but also one of admiration for my courage to do what I had done. Considering whom he was and what he was capable of doing, I was very content with my actions and finally started to feel safe, out of his weapon's range as I cornered the parking lot heading for the highway. To add insult to injury, I honked my horn just to rub it in and get him where it counted, his ego, and his lack of professional assessment dealing with an adversary. I couldn't help but think how much Greg was going to pay for what he had done to me. I just wasn't sure exactly what I would do, but I decided that it would be a good enough threat to make him think twice before doing something like that to me again.

It took nearly an hour of traveling time before the office finally came into sight. I pulled up into the driveway and saw Greg's car, so I knew he was there. His so-called office was just a small space with flimsy partitions separating him from the rest of the office in the far corner of the room. I tip-toed through the office like a cheetah stalking its prey, and then with a swift kick to his partitions, all three of them went flying down like a house of cards, leaving him totally exposed to my obvious rage.

"Oh, so you're back?" he asked casually with a little crackle in his tone and the slight hint of fear in his voice. "I guess you came back empty-handed, huh?" he added, chuckling as he spoke.

I told him that I wanted to kill him for what he had done to me, but after my enchanting conversation with Dave, I casually mentioned that I now had a professional assassin who was interested in doing it for me. His jaw dropped as though he had never considered that scenario when he sent me. Greg looked at me and suggested I just go back to Ontario where I belonged. He claimed that I didn't have the talent to survive in this province. When he saw the check for $6,000, he just gulped in shock and looked at me with surprise, saying that no one had ever gotten any money out of the guy in the past, including him.

I tried to control my temper, but it was hard. I told him that we now had $6,000 out of the $10,000 the guy owed, and I wouldn't be authorizing any future merchandise for him. I would be writing off the $4,000 balance he owed us, and if he went behind my back, I would be talking to head office about it and he could move to Ontario. As more words spewed out of my mouth, I reminded him how lucky he was that I didn't use that balance to have him disappear, and now that Dave was my good friend we had discussed that option. It, of course, was a scare tactic, but I knew it would work. I looked Greg straight in the face and told him if he wanted to mess with me again, he would have to "fuck harder or fuck off." I was surprised at my words because I wasn't one for cussing except in extreme circumstances, though this totally qualified as one of them.

Greg knew very well what he had exposed me to when he sent me there, and that's when he started looking a little worried. I could hear his oversized legs clatter against the table, so I had him where I wanted him and he knew it. Again, the power felt really good, and I loved every second of it. I just laughed the same daunting laugh that Dave gave me as I headed out of the office with the same fury I had entered with.

When Greg asked where I was going, I told him I was going home for lunch to learn French and wouldn't be back until the next morning. There was no argument as I stormed out and it was probably more of a relief for him as he watched me leave. When I got to the door, I just stared him down, telling him that he could pour gasoline on a fire with me in the middle of it, and I would find a way out, if for no other reason than simple revenge, and if he wanted to fuck with me further, he would have to do a much better job than sending me to some half-assed assassin to make that happen.

On my way home, I stopped at a music store and picked up a French teaching record. They only had Parisian-style and not Quebec-style, but I figured it was better than nothing and didn't realize exactly how much of a difference there was. Then I stopped off at the liquor store to pick up a few bottles of wine to get me through the events of the day, my French lessons, and to give me the liquid courage to face those gross warehouse jerks in the morning.

I sat and listened intently to the album, rehearsing French in front of the mirror but still shaking from my first collection with Dave and the nerve Greg had for putting me through it. I did enjoy the adrenaline rush from it all, remembering the look on Dave's face as I drove off and Greg's expression when I stormed out of his office.

I was determined to learn the language if I was going to live in Quebec, and after a few weeks of three-hour lunches, I was getting the hang of it. The only problem was the embarrassment I felt when speaking it. Every time I tried to speak to the warehouse guys, they would just laugh and make fun of me. It bugged me until I stopped trying, and in the long run, it worked in my favor. I just pretended that I didn't understand what they were saying and found out so much corrupt information to give the head office. From that point on, I researched all the law I could pertaining to Quebec business, using a dictionary to translate specific legal words into french that hobby owners would understand. I was very good at what I did, but the politics, law, and language barriers were still very frustrating.

I had had about enough of the warehouse assholes, so the next day, I called in sick and decided to go out and see the city. If I came across a bar or two, I'd have a quick drink to explore my options of how to deal with them. It was late in the day, and I was exhausted from driving around, but then I came across a bar called the "Sir Winston Churchill Pub" and parked at the back. Inside, I sat at the bar and made friends with the bartender, who spoke English, and served me a few drinks before a Scottish woman sat down beside me and introduced herself as Marion.

CHAPTER 32

Marion was a little wild, but then again, I really wasn't exactly tame myself. We spent the rest of the evening drinking together until the bar closed. I was a seasoned drinker, so the booze hadn't really affected me. When she asked for a lift home, I obliged. Her apartment was actually very close to where I lived. We made plans to go back the next night, and I was happy that I had found a new friend.

Marion entered the bar the next night around 8:00 p.m. but a few hours before she arrived, I had met an amazingly handsome man who sat on the stool next to me. His name was Anthony, and we hit it off so well before he left, that he asked me to meet him there again the next evening, and I agreed. It felt great just to be invited.

After he left, the bartender, Chad, asked me if I knew who I was just speaking with, but I had no idea, so he just stopped talking. I kept ordering more drinks with questions about this guy, but he kept his attention on other patrons. Finally, I told him that I had a $100 in my pocket if he would spill his guts and let me in on the information he was hiding.

Chad didn't tell me much except that Anthony was a regular and always had a couple of gorgeous women on his arm every time he came in. He was well respected among many high-valued individuals in the city, or so it looked when he came in with them, ordering only the best champagne, and he was one of the few millionaires who frequented this particular bar. Chad avoided answering when I asked him how he became so wealthy as if it was a secret and something that shouldn't be shared. He just figured that I was going to be one of the newest women on his arm and gave me a warning look to be careful. He went on to say that he was always there at noon when the bar opened, and if I wanted more information, I'd have to come back the next day at noon to ask him myself.

I was intrigued and arrived at noon the next day to wait for Anthony. His charisma was outstanding, and as he sat next to me, he was surprised to find me there so early. He ushered me over to his private table at the back of the bar and caressed my arm as we sat and talked. I was no fool about these kinds of men, so the conversation was always directed toward him. After two bottles of bubbly, he asked if I would accompany him back to his place to continue the party. I agreed and exited the bar on his arm with Chad staring at me as we left. It was still eight hours before I was to meet Marion, and a little romance would do me wonders and give me something to talk about. It had been a very long time since I had been with a man, and to say Anthony was gorgeous was an understatement.

We pulled up to this monstrous Victorian home that I couldn't stop staring at as he got out of the car with one of his "butlers" opening the door for me. I tried to pretend that his money didn't matter and just casually commented that he had a nice home. When he asked if I would like a tour, I looked at my watch, monitoring the time. It impressed him that I wasn't interested too much in his home like the other women were. He would just give me a quick tour before heading to his bedroom. I agreed but couldn't help but notice the incredibly detailed architecture as we entered. It obviously cost him a fortune and more money than I would ever make in a lifetime.

After the most amazing sex I think I ever had, his phone rang, and he jumped to answer it. He hung up, and I thought it was just another one of his women friends on the other end, but he looked stressed at the content of the call. The look on his face told a story that something had happened and was seriously wrong. He quickly explained that he had to leave as soon as possible and ran off to the bathroom for a quick shower. I sat baffled and asked if everything was okay. All he said was that there was a family meeting he had to attend and that it was about to start.

He instructed me to get dressed and said his driver would drive me home. As I got up, I noticed his pants at my feet, so I decided to search inside his wallet for some kind of ID. Nothing seemed right with what he was saying. What kind of serious family meeting could it be? He told me in the bar that his last name was Castro, but as I quickly searched his wallet, I found his driver's license claiming his name was actually Castrogiovali. I returned the wallet and quickly dressed, trying to return everything perfectly the way I found it, and not over-thinking the lie he just told me.

I didn't understand why he felt he had to lie to me about such a thing, so, when his driver dropped me at home, I ran upstairs to my computer to Google his name. To my shock and surprise, the Castrogiovali family controlled most of Montreal, and Anthony too was highly connected to the Italian Mafia. He was apparently a hit man for them, and I wasn't sure why he was with me unless he followed me from Toronto and planned to kill me.

I freaked at my incredibly bad luck, remembering the reason I was in Montreal. Now, this guy knew me and where I lived. I tried to take a nap before meeting

Marion but couldn't sleep, thinking about what I had just done and how long it would take before they discovered who I was, or if they already knew. There were too many articles on the web of the horrific things that this Mafia had done to people; murder, extortion, blackmail, drugs, prostitution, and list went on. It was understandable why he lied to me about his name, but then again, Anthony didn't know that I rifled through his wallet while he was in the shower, or had he? My mind was racing, wondering whether I had put his ID back exactly where I had found it and the consequences of what would happen to me if I didn't. I made my way toward the Sir Winston Churchill Pub to meet Marion, looking over my shoulder at every street corner and alleyway. I was scared to death thinking he might already know who I was, or maybe toying with me until he would find the right time and place to kill me.

Marion had already been sitting there when I arrived, but she could tell that there was something weighing heavily on my mind. I combed through each of her words trying to figure out if Anthony had sent her there because of who I was, so I told her that I just had the most amazing sex with a man I had just met there a few hours earlier and watched her every expression as I spoke.

She looked at me as if she was very interested, and I guessed that she felt she knew me well enough that she could actually talk to me about personal stuff too. It opened up a whole different dialogue, and she was very forthcoming in a descriptive detail about her indiscretions since she arrived in Montreal three years previously. Of course, I listened intently, looking for more information, and by the end of the night, I figured that she was either really good at lying, or she was actually true to who she was, and had absolutely nothing to do with Anthony or the Mafia.

Marion and I spent most nights at the pub, having a great time and talking about everything. I felt comfortable telling her about my past and why I was there, making her promise not to tell a living soul. I predicted death in my near future by the mob anyway, and I knew from Toronto that it was just a question of time, so it didn't really matter at this point. She surprised me by swearing to secrecy and asked if I would do the same about her life, which was nothing compared to mine, but very important to her just the same. We laughed and became even better friends. I hadn't heard back from Anthony for quite awhile. I went home that night after closing the bar with Marion to find him sitting in my apartment waiting for me. Shit!

I was shocked to find him there, but he politely told me that I needed to move to a higher apartment because when his car was parked in the driveway below, it was an easy grab to the trellis from the hood of his car to get onto my balcony, and a quick pick to unlock my balcony door.

He told me that he missed me, but from what I had read in the newspapers, I was hesitant to believe any explanation. He told me he knew I had gone into his wallet and was happy that I never took out any of the cash inside. He thought I was genuine with my interest in him and that I was just being a cautious woman, which impressed him. I wanted him to leave more than anything, but I knew how dangerous he was, so I would agree to anything just so he would go.

With genuine care, he told me that he had to get out of town for awhile and asked if I would be there for him when he returned. Without hesitation, I caressed his face, hoping that he wouldn't notice my hands shaking and told him that I would look forward to when he returned, no questions asked, and we could be together for a very long time.

He kissed me with the most passionate kiss, telling me that I wasn't like those whores his father forced him to be seen with in public. I relaxed a little, wondering if he was being honest and then collapsed into his arms, hoping that he wouldn't pull a gun out and shoot me in the head. I just played dumb, but I could tell that he appreciated my honesty with what he thought I knew about him. Across the room, I noticed that my computer was opened to the page where I had researched him, and there was no doubt in my mind that I had closed my computer out before meeting Marion earlier in the evening. As soon as he left, I would put a password on my computer just as a precaution for the future.

Before he left, he kissed my forehead one more time, and then he walked toward the balcony, leaving the same way he came. He jumped over the railing onto his car parked below, and when I heard the thump as he hit the hood, I forced myself to keep away from the door just in case he changed his mind. A few minutes later, I heard the car drive away, and relief filled my body. I was still thinking of the hell that had just happened and how thankful I was to still be alive.

I couldn't believe my luck, leaving behind so much trouble in Toronto, and then within a few short months, I had gone from bad to worse with the mob again. I laid my head down on the sofa without pulling it out into a bed and fell into a dreamless sleep until my alarm went off in the morning. Then I dressed and headed to the office.

I sat at my desk wondering if Anthony actually hunted me down from Toronto, but he had every opportunity to kill me so many times and didn't do it. He only showed genuine care and love toward me, so those terrible thoughts soon left my mind. I was sure that Anthony would be the one to kill me if the contract came up, and I sat contemplating every word he had ever said to me. Fear had always been a part of my life, so I relaxed a little, thinking that maybe he told his father that he had already killed me and this would be as far as it would go.

I was still terrified with what I had gotten myself involved with, so I always searched the bar for anyone new staring at me. It wasn't easy with several men coming up to me each night, asking me to dance, and then asking me to meet them later. Of course, I turned them all down, and as us girls closed the bar again, I repeatedly asked Chad to escort me to my car. He was huge and burley, attractive in many ways, and a body-builder, so I felt safe with him. Each night, he would wave to me as I drove off the parking lot, but getting back to my apartment was another story. I had to move elsewhere soon, and I knew it. Anthony told me to move for a reason, and maybe it was because the mob knew where I lived now. Since my relationships never worked out very well for me, I wondered what the mob would do to Anthony if they found out he confided in me about his business, if his bosses knew that we were seeing each other, and if they knew I was still alive or if I even existed. I still hadn't seen or heard anything from him since the night he broke into my apartment.

It was two weeks later when I heard on the news that Anthony had been brutally tortured and murdered, and his body found in an isolated ditch at the top of the Montreal Mountain by a jogger. I was terrified at what he was tortured into telling them. At work, I told Greg I needed another apartment higher up in the building and that someone had broken into my place being so close to the parking right below me. I said that it needed to happen *now*. Luckily, a resident had just vacated, and her apartment on the fifth floor at the back of the building was now free. I took it immediately and the moving truck was there within the hour to move my belongings.

Several months after the news of Anthony's death and me still being alive, I finally thought that my fear had come to an end. Then, I was driving to a client's one evening and I recognized one of the men from court that the judge said was there to kill me if I didn't take the rap for their drugs. I passed by him with my head turned away and took a right at the next corner, where I pulled over and gave it a lot of thought. Was it possible that they had finally found me? I quickly turned the next corner again to do another drive-by to see if it really was him, but he had disappeared. Greg had put my apartment in the company name after the break-in so that helped. I drove around for an hour before going home, checking my rearview mirror often as I pulled into the driveway. Everything seemed to be fine, so I ran up the stairs to my apartment and checked my front door for anything out of the ordinary. After Anthony broke in that night, I started leaving a strand of my hair jammed into the door in an inconspicuous spot no one would notice. When the door was opened, the hair would fall out of its spot, and I would be able to tell if anyone had broken in. So far so good!

The next day, I went to work terrified that it would only be a matter of time before they found me. Mid day I had an idea so I got up and headed downtown to my hairdresser's to have my hair cut as short as possible and styled completely different. I also had it dyed a deep black over my blond hair to try and evade detection. I bound my breasts as tight as I could, and hadn't been eating well in weeks, so I was smaller than I was that day in court. After all was done, I was physically unrecognizable, except for my voice. I had been practicing a southern accent from a television show that would throw anyone off when they spoke to me. This was the last chance I had to reclaim my life, so I had to make it work. I changed my look so much that when I went back to work a couple of days later, no one in the office recognized me. Greg, of course, questioned me about the change, but I just told him that it was something between Damien and me that he wasn't privy to. Then I called Damien and told him everything just in case Greg called. Damien was very concerned and asked if I would reconsider him talking to the bosses who too were Mafia affiliated. The last thing I wanted was a mob war, so I respectfully declined, also mentioning that he had come this far with me and my secrets, and to please not let me down at this point. He was about the only person I really trusted, probably because we both had secrets that neither of us wanted revealed.

I continued meeting Marion almost every night at the pub. She worked for the government's External Affairs Division, so she had flexible hours and was always there when I arrived. Even Marion hadn't recognized me when I entered the bar, and of course with my southern accent, she was sure that I was just some friendly female looking for some kind of conversation. I changed my drink order when Chad asked, and every person known to me knew I hated beer, so it was now my drink of choice, and I sat nursing the disgusting taste until closing. I had to be vigilant with absolutely everything I did, so staying sober could just possibly save my life.

Things at work were going extremely well, and somehow, I managed to clear the receivables from $800,000 outstanding to $30,000 in only thirteen months. Everyone, including head office in Toronto, was thrilled at my ability to collect the money owed in such a short period of time and gave me a huge bonus for doing it. My company was almost out of the red with a foreseeable future.

Greg and I became very close, and we started dating to the point that I felt very uncomfortable being with him. He was short, bald, and had such a huge belly on him, but he actually cared a lot about me, so much so, that it was a very hard to let him know I was no longer interested. He had given me everything I wanted and even what I didn't want; with gifts, compliments, and lots of company expense money. I wasn't the relationship type anymore with all I had gone through in my life, so it inevitably didn't last very long. The engagement ring was the show stopper, and I had to let him down gently. He was still my boss, but I knew I couldn't tell him my predicament. Damien warned me to keep my mouth shut, and I wasn't going to blow it.

After moving to another apartment in the building, I had the best security system installed that money could buy and a lifeline medallion I wore around my neck under my shirt just as an extra precaution. I wasn't ready to die at age twenty-four.

Although Marion and I loved the Sir Winston Churchill Pub, we had found another bar to frequent, and I was actually feeling the safest I had felt in a long time. It was a seedy little bar, but I knew that the types of people looking for me wouldn't even think of going to such a dive. I tried several times to sway Marion from staying my friend just because I feared for her life too, and considering what had happened to Anthony with his horrific murder, it wasn't worth it to me to have my one and only friend die the same kind of death because of me. Marion would just laugh at the thought and told me what a roller-coaster ride it was having me as a friend and that she wouldn't give it up for the world. That was Marion, and I loved her for her sense of adventure, but she was also very naïve at what the world was really like. She was definitely a thrill seeker, but at the same time, I wasn't quite sure if she really understood the consequences of having me as a friend.

There wasn't much I wasn't good at, but this Mafia thing hanging over my head was absolutely exhausting, pretending to be a totally different person and always being on my guard twenty-four/seven with no margin for error.

The bar Marion and I were frequenting was being closed down by the health department so we decided to go back to the Sir Winston Churchill Pub. So much time had passed since we had been there last, and it was a risk that we both agreed to try again. It had really changed with so many different faces now, mostly younger university types, so anyone else would have stuck out like a sore thumb, and I liked that.

It was the week before Halloween, 1981, when a nice-looking man about my same age came up and asked me to dance. I thought he looked innocent enough with his handsome, baby-like face, so I agreed, but while I was walking behind him to the dance floor, some woman purposely tripped me, and I fell to the floor. Apparently, she liked this same man and had been dating him for awhile. He claimed to have broken it off with her, but it was obvious that she was still terribly jealous at my attempt to dance with him, and was anything but shy in letting me know it. Well, I waited for this guy to do something about it, and when he didn't, I shoved her back flat onto her face, and she hit the floor. Chad interceded and threw her out of the bar, warning her never to come back again. This was nothing compared to what I was used to, so I just continued to the dance floor as if nothing had happened. The guy apologized for her rudeness, saying it was the reason he stopped seeing her. We had a nice dance, although he was terrible at it, but we sat later drinking together until it was time to go home.

CHAPTER 33

His name was Tom, and he was very polite, innocent looking, obviously educated, and he offered me a ride home. For the first time since I started coming to the bar, I had actually walked there that night, so I graciously accepted, thinking that maybe it was fate with all the excitement that happened over the course of the evening.

When we exited the bar, we walked through the parking lot while I tried to figure out which of the cars he was driving. As we talked, he told me that he was a student at the university, and all I could think about was if this relationship would go anywhere, I would be supporting him through school, and I certainly didn't need a dependent at this time in my life. Then, he stopped at this gorgeous Z28 black beauty with a T-bar roof, obviously brand new and worth a lot of money, so the statement he said about being a student didn't make much sense. I got into the car just the same, and we drove up to the front of my building, where he dropped me off. He was being coy and told me if I was interested in him to come back to the pub the next weekend on Halloween for us to continue whatever it was that we were doing together. He made no advances toward me, nor did he ask for my phone number, and that impressed me.

I thought about it, but it was Marion who actually talked me into going back to meet him again. She was sure that this was going to be my opportunity at real love and to finally have a solid relationship that would go somewhere.

To be honest, I never thought that far ahead into my future, knowing I could be dead at any time, but I did show up that night, and to my surprise, Tom never came. I just guessed that he had another date and that would be the end of it. It did intrigue me though, since every other guy I dated from the pub was an asshole, looking for a one-night stand, so I just shook them off the second they made their move. I still couldn't believe Tom had such a great car being a university student, and I gave it a lot of thought until I saw him again at the pub. Now, I had my chance to probe further into whom he really was and why he stood me up.

It had been two weeks since the drive home when he arrived at the pub and spotted me on my usual stool with Marion. He casually stopped by, apologizing for not showing up Halloween night with no real excuse, so I just waved him off as if I wasn't interested in any bullshit lie he could conjure up. He came alone and asked if he could sit with us. Marion, of course, was nudging me to accept his apology, which I didn't appreciate, but I was still cordial toward him. Then Marion said she had a previous engagement and had to leave, getting up without so much as finishing her drink, and before I knew it, she was gone and I was left sitting with this guy who had already stood me up once.

I was about to leave too when a slow song came on and he asked me to dance. Again, he apologized emphatically, saying that he had a family matter that popped up and he had no choice but to go. He was sorry that he didn't take my phone number down that night, and that was the reason he wasn't able to call and cancel. I told him that I forgave him, blah, blah, blah, and I guess I made it very obvious that it was a really lame excuse that I wasn't falling for.

After rejecting his invitation to dance, I got up to leave when he took my arm gently and kissed me on the lips, telling me that he wanted to get to know me better. It was a warm and loving kiss that I couldn't refuse, and I kissed him back with the same amount of passion. At the end of the night, we left together, heading to his apartment close by the bar; obvious that we would spend the night together.

On the drive to his place, he apparently didn't

remember telling me that he was a student, because, in fact, he was an engineer for a well-known aviation company in Quebec. He had been there for several months after just graduating university and made a great salary. I made like I didn't care when actually I was relieved that he had a reputable job that could be in no way connected to any kind of mob affiliation. He seemed to be perfect for me, and as I viewed his apartment, I could see the aviation books lining his shelves, which convinced me he actually was who he said he was.

We dated several weeks before he asked me to move in with him. That was great because I needed to move away from my building just as a precaution, so I accepted his invitation, warning myself to be careful because he was the kind of man I could easily fall in love with. While we were courting, I would cook a nice meal, but when he came home, he didn't just bring one bottle of wine for dinner; he brought three or four which I thought was a little excessive, and then polished them off mostly by himself. I was known to polish off a few bottles myself in one night, but with my lifestyle and history, I never considered myself as an alcoholic. I just drank to forget, so I wondered what his story was that made him drink so much. Weeks had passed with our heavy drinking habits, only to find that when we were drunk, our personalities clashed so much that I stopped drinking completely, hoping he would do the same but with no such luck.

After ten months of our living together, he asked me to marry him. We visited his parents for the first time the next night. They were nice people of European descent, and both alcoholics, so it started to make sense why Tom drank as much as he did. I hit it off with his parents within minutes of meeting them, but it was getting late, and they all had too much to drink, so it was time to leave. I had to be at work early the following day, so Tom agreed to leave and convinced me he was sober enough to drive.

As we were leaving, he got into his Z28, but instead of reversing the car out of the driveway, he drunkenly put the car in drive and destroyed his father's garage where his prized Cadillac was parked. I was on the porch with his mother saying good-bye when it happened and then just looked at her pleadingly for her not to let him drive me home in his drunken condition.

That didn't work well, probably because his parents were more inebriated than he was, but we stayed for a couple more coffees before getting up to leave, and Tom seemed to have sobered up enough that I felt safe driving with him.

The problem was that his car was a standard transmission, and I had never learned how to drive a stick, so somehow, it became my fault. I just chalked it up to all the alcohol, and the next time we went there for dinner, nothing was said, and the garage door and Cadillac were fixed as if it had never happened.

I liked his parents probably because they weren't anything like mine at all. I felt comfortable with them, but the excessive drinking was something I didn't like since I had quit, and that was probably the reason why I noticed it more. They were friendly and loving parents, maybe not toward each other but toward their son, and I liked that about them. They had a reputable electronics company, so they worked all day together and lived at night in a tiny, modest bungalow. I knew that it must have been very hard on any marriage and the reason they drank so much. Then they mentioned that they had a winter home down south, and somehow, it made the arguments they had go away to the point that I could tolerate their intemperate style of family life. It didn't take much to start seeing myself as being fortunate to have the opportunity to live such a normal life, to have beautiful children and never have to worry about the terrible things I ran from in my life, and now there would be no money problems and no dreadful people chasing me anymore.

Life was good for the first five years. We had two beautiful boys, with our first-born being Brent, and then Adam, almost exactly two years apart. Unfortunately, with my spine disease and the rods in my back holding my spine together, both the pregnancies were horrific and painful. It was then that Tom changed for the worse. He was always away on business, sometimes for four to six months at a time, and having the ability to speak three languages fluently, he was a definite asset to his company, and they used him like a tool.

In contrast, I was at home with two babies in diapers with no relief whatsoever while he was gone, and slowly started drinking again in the evenings. When he was home, he was distant, and no matter what I did, it wasn't good enough for him. Many times, he went away on a business trip and would forget to leave me money or a credit card for necessities like food and diapers, so my mother would come to my rescue. She still lived in Toronto while we were in Montreal, and at her age, the train trip was very draining, but I very much appreciated her coming. I doubt if the boys and I could have survived without her help.

The damage to my spine from the babies during pregnancy required more surgery, and I think that was when Tom started seeing me more as a liability than an adequate wife and mother. The rods in my back were broken from the babies' weight lying on them, and the pain was unbearable.

My fairytale marriage and hope for a promising future started to fade quickly with each year, and then each month. I was free from the Mafia looking for me since I had changed my name after we got married, and I tried to hold onto that relief if nothing else. What I wasn't prepared for was what would soon become of me and another terrible nightmare I couldn't imagine, as it unfolded.

The wait for surgery was eighteen months in Montreal, and I wouldn't survive that long with such severe pain. There were only a few heavy narcotic drugs capable of helping, but the eighties were manipulated by an epidemic of opiate abusers, so the best meds I could get were Tylenol #3s from the sorry-ass doctor my husband recommended me to; *his* doctor.

Tom's doctor didn't believe in being a part of the problem, only a part of the solution, so he refused to prescribe the heavy meds for me I knew would work. Why I was viewed as part of the problem with my medical history was baffling. There were growing guidelines and restrictions for physicians prescribing narcotics if they wanted to keep their licenses, especially given to those patients who professed in needing them as badly as I did. Since I was a brand-new patient, he wasn't interested in my medical history, which was always available to him, validating my complaint, and yet, he never tried. He only saw me as one of those loser users, leaving me to sit at the bottom of his suffering pile, almost proud of himself for thinking he was saving another addicted junkie.

Somehow, I felt that Tom was responsible for me being treated like this by his doctor. When his cell phone bill came in, I found several calls from him to his doctor when he never had a visit or any reason to call. Those calls all lined up within a day before my visit, the day of, and then the day after I went to see him, so I couldn't help but consider the possibility.

I just kept my cool without confronting him, wondering how a man could watch the woman he swore to love in sickness and in health, be witness to so much of my suffering without doing anything about it. I guess that was one of the signs I should have recognized with the gradual deterioration of our marriage over the next six years, and the malicious monster he was becoming. His sinister behavior had my sister's contribution written all over it, but his obvious hatred for her convinced me that it wasn't plausible, and so I disregarded the thought. That was a huge mistake on my part because I felt it clear with every bone in my body that she was somehow behind it!

Then an opportunity came up for Tom to change companies and move over to their competitors in the US. This would allow us to move to Arizona, where surgery could be done after three months when our benefits kicked in. We were both happy about the move until I went to a psychic and was told that it would be the worst thing that I could ever possibly do in my lifetime. He repeatedly warned me not to go, and was actually frightened for me with so much I should be concerned about. I didn't take it too seriously with everything I knew about my husband from the time we met, and how innocent his life was compared to mine. Tom was a good provider; we had beautiful upscale homes, but I also felt that my husband wouldn't transfer thousands of miles away, to another country, just for me, and I was right. Tom always hated Canadian winters and the thought of the Arizona sun had to be a major factor in his decision to take the job.

The job and move were already in the works, before any consideration was made toward me, so I didn't have much of a choice but to go. I would have to move forward regardless of what the psychic said, but I would always try to keep what he said first and foremost in my mind. I hoped that moving to the sun-filled state of Arizona would be a new start for Tom and me, so I focused on that as being something very positive. I also thought of my sister and that moving farther away from her, I would somehow finally be safer from her cruelty. Unfortunately, it wasn't her cruelty I had to be afraid of in the future, although the few times she did try, she failed. There was another monster evolving that I never expected and too blind to see at the time, but now he was becoming my subjugator no matter how hard I tried to focus on the positive.

Of course, psychics were not always right with their predictions, and when he also told me that I would have another baby, a baby girl this time, within the next four years, I started to doubt his predictions. It completely took me by surprise with my unstable spine, and Tom refusing to have another child when our marriage was rapidly deteriorating. His predictions didn't make much sense until it all unfolded a couple of years later. The move was, in fact, the worst mistake I could have ever made, and I was heading to a hell I couldn't control or escape from.

CHAPTER 34

Tom was a clean freak, and on one occasion, after I had finished cleaning the sparkling white kitchen he insisted on having when the house was built, he would humiliate me by cleaning it again right afterward, just to degrade me when friends came over. They would compliment him on how clean and beautiful our house was, making sure they knew it was him who cleaned it, and then shooting me a look of disgust.

I used to take my diamond wedding rings off when I cleaned with bleach and other astringent cleaners. Only this one time when I went to put them back on, they had somehow disappeared. I was frantic, thinking they had been accidently flushed down the kitchen drain, but I was too afraid to tell Tom about it. The next day, while he was at work, I called a plumber who came and removed the entire pipe under the sink, swearing that if they had gone into the drain, he would find them in the elbow of the pipe. They were nowhere to be found, so I thanked him and paid for his services from the few dollars I was pilfering from the grocery money so Tom wouldn't find out. A couple of days later, I was cleaning out our closets, and while I was moving one of his shoes to vacuum, to my surprise, both my rings fell out of his shoe. I was furious but kept my cool, and I never mentioned it. I just put the rings back on my finger and carried on with my cleaning.

It wasn't more than a week later when Tom all of a sudden insisted that I clean all the shelving surfaces in our three-car garage. I thought it very weird, because who does that in a garage, unless it is really filthy? Tom usually did that when he felt it was necessary, but this time he brought in a new cleaner from his car that he claimed to have just bought, and when I went to get my rubber gloves, they were nowhere to be found. I was always so organized because Tom claimed that "everything had its place in the house." Anything else he didn't like would quickly disappear, whether I liked it or not. When I told him I needed to go to the store first to buy gloves, he ordered me to get the job done immediately with no apparent justification and pushed me toward the garage. I thought, *"What the hell?"*, and started cleaning his damned garage. It had taken me three hours with his specific instructions, and I had only gotten one-third of the garage finished. It was a Friday, and he would be home the entire weekend to supervise me finishing it before he went back to work on Monday. This didn't make any sense to me whatsoever because he always played golf with his friends religiously on weekends for the entire day. To avoid further problems, I did what he asked, working hard and hoping to finish the job by Monday.

It was Sunday night when I started to feel terribly ill. I was dizzy, vomiting and had constant diarrhea. I had black circles forming under my eyes, and my nails looked really strange with discolored horizontal lines across them that I never had before. I was so weak that I couldn't do anything but stay in bed, and Tom was furious as usual with my behavior, bitching now about how inept I was as a wife and the mother of his children. Of course, I apologized like a good wife and said that I would go to the doctor in the morning. He was furious that he would have to pay for a babysitter and leave his children with a stranger because I was too stupid to take care of myself. I was scared that something was seriously wrong with me but told him not to worry and that I would wait a few days to see if I would get better. That didn't happen, and I just got worse until I could barely walk. Meanwhile, he insisted that I clean the walkway that went from the front of the house and circled around to the back with the same cleaner, but without the strength to do it, I lied to him about how much I did.

By the next Friday, I couldn't take it any longer and had my girlfriend care for the kids while I crawled to the clinic. The doctor asked questions, and without any conclusive answers, he took a blood test. I had lost so much weight over the past two weeks that when he weighed me on the scales at eighty-seven pounds, I actually became very concerned.

When Tom came home that night, I decided to tell him that I went to the doctor, and he insisted on taking a blood test. Of course, Tom was furious with me for not consulting him first. I excused myself after dinner, telling him I would finish cleaning the back patio in an attempt to make the rest of the night bearable between us when he stopped me, saying he would do it himself. I was grateful not to have to do it, at least until after the Wednesday when the doctor said he would call. Thankfully, the call came during the day when Tom was at work. He proceeded to tell me that were was an unidentified substance in my blood and asked me to come back for another blood test, searching for various toxins he never thought to test me for the first time. Of course, I told Tom after the phone call, and for the first time, he looked worried about something. He caringly told me to go and lie down and said he would bring me lots of fluids necessary to flush out whatever might be in my system. He was very emphatic about it so I went to bed while he doted on me and cared for the children for the first time in seven years. I should have seen the signs, but I never would have expected anything like this from him or what was about to happen.

On the Thursday when I went back to the doctor again, he took another blood test. He called me a few days later, telling me that there was still a trace of some unknown toxin in my system, but not enough to identify. When I told him that I was feeling better, he was happy to hear it but still sounded concerned. I told him that my husband had started taking very good care of me during my illness, and that was when the doctor told me to be very careful and to call him the following week if I got worse. I didn't understand what he was trying to tell me, but red flags were rising, and I became very aware that something was going on that wasn't right, never considering the possibility of being poisoned.

CHAPTER 35

The poisoning eventually surfaced and made sense when Tom presented me with divorce papers a few days later. I started searching through his office desk, looking for answers, and trying to find out where he hid all of his millions. That's when I found that Tom had taken out a 1.5 million-dollar insurance policy on me behind my back. It was a state law that for any policy exceeding $250,000, it required the insured's signature in the presence of the insurance agent, which never happened. I wasn't going to go easy now with all he had put me through over the years, and I wanted more than fair compensation for it. I just wasn't expecting murder to be his alternative to a divorce and never thought he was even capable of something so devious. I was in over my head, and I knew it, but the one thing he never figured on was the life I used to have before him, how smart I was to survive it, and how thankful I was that I had never told him anything about it before we got married.

I wasn't about to call the police and draw attention to myself with my past, just in case that court thing didn't completely disappear and I ended up in prison for those drug charges. Tom would have just loved if that had happened, and I wouldn't give him the satisfaction. I was so livid that I called the insurance agent who wrote the fraudulent policy and threatened to turn him in as a co-conspirator. I also threatened him that if he called Tom and told him about our phone call that he would also be charged as an accessory to attempted murder and I would make sure that his entire life would be ripped apart. After he swore not to tell, I hung up the phone and continued photocopying the files I needed from Tom's desk.

It wasn't five minutes later when I heard Tom's car screeching to a stop in the driveway and the front door flying open. I quickly put everything back into the drawer and walked into the hallway to greet him as if everything was normal with a smile on my face. That took him by surprise, as he pushed by me and told me that he had work to do in his office, and locked the door behind him. I knocked on the door calmly, but he refused to answer so I started yelling at him to open the door. There was too little time to photocopy the entire policy, and as he continued to ignore me, I could hear the paper shredder going at full speed. I knew then that the insurance agent had called him, and now I was screwed for the evidence that would put them both away.

I went to the kitchen phone and called the agent, but it went to voice mail so I called back, asking for the agent's manager. When he came on the phone, I calmly asked for him to pull up my insurance policy, giving him the reference number, and hoping he could mail me a copy. I was put on hold for several minutes until he returned, telling me that there was no such policy written up under the number I gave him. Damn, they were good. The policy had been written only a few days prior to the garage cleaning incident, so, either it hadn't been entered into their computer yet or the salesman had second thoughts about its validity. I was confused and frustrated at not being able to tell who all was involved and working with Tom. It was so well orchestrated and executed, and I'm guessing in the event that my "stupidity" managed to uncover their scheme, they had this plan in place all along to destroy the evidence at both ends. I was totally helpless, and now I had lost all hope to prove Tom to be the monster and murderer he truly was. When Tom came out of his office, he just loomed over me, pushing me aside, heading for the front door, and saying he had to go back to work. The office door was locked, but I took my art tools from our library, and a half-hour later, I was able to pick the lock. When I entered, I ran straight to the closet where I stashed most of the files that I did manage to copy before he came home, and they were gone. When I opened his desk drawer, all of his financial papers were gone too, so he must have put them in his briefcase when he left the house. After checking the shredder, I noticed that it too was empty and he had taken the paper from there as well. My mind was racing as I cried at the kitchen table, wondering what to do next. I decided my only option was to wait until he came home after work and fell asleep, steal his briefcase, and remove his files. Better yet, I would steal the briefcase and bury it in the backyard where he wouldn't find it and in the morning take the kids and move out. I was disgusted in myself for letting this happen. My entire life revolved around evil like this, dealing with so many adversaries trying to hurt, or annihilate me, and I never saw this coming. Flashbacks of my life quickly zoomed into focus, and then I thought about my children. Tom never cared about them until he tried to kill me, and I couldn't help but think he would try to kill them too.

When he got home after work, unlike the past nine years when he brought his briefcase with him, he didn't have it now. He didn't speak a word to me the entire night, so after I put the kids to bed, I tried to get up enough nerve to say something to him about it, but he just went to bed at eight, taking a bottle of wine with him as he went. I should have never called the agent, and I should have been more careful, never considering Tom was capable of doing such a hideous thing. I stayed alert on the sofa all night, thinking how deranged he was, and worried that he might try to kill me again during the night with a newly fabricated story ready to tell police.

The next day, he got up before the kids, dressed for work, and told me that he was moving out to a motel until he could find an apartment. I just nodded and said, "Good luck with that." Three days later, a moving truck showed up at the house, and removed all of the furniture he had before we got married and then tried to take some of mine, which I refused to allow. I was thankful that the kids were at school and didn't see what was going on. When I asked him what I was supposed to tell our children, he certainly didn't look too concerned. He just flicked his hand at me and said, "I don't give a damn what you tell them, and they aren't my children anyway." After that repulsive comment, I knew that he was out of his mind, and capable of anything. I was glad he was gone!

Later in the day, he called and told me that he had found an apartment and I needed to take the kids and quickly get out of the house because he was selling it, and we had to go. After we hung up, I started to cry. Tom was always so cheap with his precious millions, and now he was leaving me and his children destitute. I had been pilfering little bits of money from the leftover grocery money for several months, but it certainly wasn't enough to put a deposit down or first and last month's rent on an apartment. I had nothing to my name except the furniture I fought to keep and my two children he obviously didn't want.

I refused to believe that Tom would sell the house while his family was still living in it, but the next few days proved me wrong when the utility companies cut off the water, electricity, and heat. I was mortified and scared to death, mostly for our children, whom he had abandoned. It was February in the desert with daytime temperatures reaching triple digits some days, and the night-time temperatures dipping below zero. Without heat or the use of the heavy blankets Tom took with him, the children would freeze.

While the kids were in school, I headed out to find an apartment. There was a complex not too far from us, and luckily they had a two-bedroom that was available immediately. While I was filling out the paperwork in the office, the manager asked me why I was moving, and reminded me that I also needed references from work, and a financial report. When I told him I was getting divorced, I didn't have a job, and I only had a US green card, he just shook his head. Apparently, in the early nineties in Arizona, divorced women were too high of a risk, and it was their company policy not to accept their applications, especially those holding a green card. I promised him that my husband was wealthy, and once the divorce was finalized, he would have everything he needed. He just shook his head again, asking if I had any collateral. I thought for a few minutes and then remembered my RRSP from Canada that had over $20,000 in the account. I knew that I wasn't able to access that money until I turned sixty-five, but the manager wasn't too bright, and it was my only hope to convince him that it was a valid document he could use. He hummed and hawed, asking to see the paperwork, so I told him to hold the apartment with a hundred dollars I had from grocery money, and I would be back in ten minutes with the bank statement. He agreed, and I ran home to get it. Tom hadn't turned the phone off yet, so I called and told him that I had found an apartment, but because I had no job and no money, he was going to have to pay the first and last month's rent. To my surprise, he agreed and promised to drop the check off to the manager after work. In the meantime, I found my RRSP statement and ran back to the complex. I handed it to the manager and waited for him to make a copy, and a decision. When I told him that my husband would be dropping off his check after work, it seemed to satisfy him. Of course, Tom never told me where his new apartment was, so it made a lot of sense when I found out he had moved into the same apartment complex, and why the manager agreed so quickly.

The manager called that evening to confirm receipt of the check, so I called the moving company to arrange the furniture pickup and delivery for the next day. I also called Tom, and it nearly killed me to thank him for the check, but the boys and I were not going to survive without food, necessities, and money, so I asked him what he planned to do about it.

Of course, he had that all figured out as well, because within seconds, he told me to check our mailbox. He had gotten a prepaid credit card for the things I asked for, and it was there waiting for me. The boys of course didn't have a clue what was happening, and with their father not there, I simply told them that he was away on business again, and that the house was being renovated. It seemed to temporarily satisfy their curiosity, while surrounded in packed boxes, but I was going to have to tell them the truth very soon. They had already witnessed the constant fighting between us but never expected that we would be moving from our mansion into a tiny two-bedroom apartment. They would just have to adjust, and it was up to me to make the transition, as smooth as possible, if it wasn't going to impact them with serious emotional consequences.

The next day, while they were at school, the movers came and delivered the furniture, leaving the apartment in total chaos with only five hours for me to organize and set everything up before the kids got home from school. It was hard, and with my spine, it was terribly painful, but I managed to do it. I called the school to change the bus drop-off to the apartment instead of the house, and I was there to meet them when the bus came. The look on their poor faces hurt me so badly inside, but I greeted them with a smile and sat them down in our new apartment, breaking the news to them as gently as possible.

They were mortified when I told them, and they had more questions than I had answers for. The one thing they did like was that our apartment was situated right next to a gorgeous swimming pool that was much bigger than the one we had at home. They noticed the many kids their same age at the pool, and they didn't have friends at the house, so they were happy with that. I showed them the room they would have to share with their bathing suits and towels laying neatly across both their beds. It didn't take much convincing when I told them to go out and meet some great kids at the pool, which they were happy to do.

I started making supper, expecting more questions when they came in with such solemn looks on their faces, staring at the dinner table, and it took my breath away. I made them pork chops with mashed

potatoes and carrots, their favorite foods, but neither of them ate anything. I had to do something to cheer them up, remembering at home the strict regimen their father demanded at mealtime; with no fooling around and having to finish all of their food before leaving the table.

Out of the blue, I took my spoon and flicked some of the mashed potatoes at both of them, instigating a food fight. It literally freaked them both out at what I had done. I told them that things were different now, and we had to christen our new home. They paused for a minute, and then they both got into it too. The mess was terrible, but worth it. Afterward, they got up and saw some of the kids they met earlier at the pool, and ran out to play.

Months passed by as they got used to our new apartment. They met some really nice kids, and things seemed to be settling down. We had no money except for the little Tom controlled, so I started thinking of a business I could start that wouldn't require much of a set-up fee. I only had my car, my wits, and my survival skills, so, I put them together and "Ahwatukee Courier and Delivery Service" was created. I called my mom and told her what had happened to us and my plans for the company I just started. She flew down to Arizona and stayed with us, and then she put up the money to start my business. I needed a cell phone badly for the job, and back then, the Motorola cell phones were enormous and very expensive. I also needed brochures made up, and she paid for them as well. We were out shopping one day when a stationery store display caught our eye. They had these cute funny ink stamps in the window, so we went in. There was one with a woman struggling with grocery bags and books, so mom suggested it would be a cute logo for my new company, and I agreed.

I spent hours every day and night calling companies to promote my business, and I was getting very good at it. It was exhausting until I finally found a florist who needed my services. I had no idea what to charge them, but we eventually negotiated a six-dollar fee for me to deliver each bouquet or plant, and although it didn't seem like much, the deliveries were plentiful, and they were impressed with my work. I was now in business, and word of the superb services I offered at a great price was getting well known within the community.

I finally started making good money, but I was still up almost twenty-two hours a day trying to build it bigger and better with other local businesses. I barely knew Phoenix so I bought a road map to familiarize myself with the area, but it was still difficult with all the new developments rapidly growing that weren't yet on the map.

I was surprised one evening, when out of the blue,

Chloe, dropped by the apartment. She was the wife of one of Tom's work friends. We were all supposed to go out to a bar one night until Tom bowed out, claiming he was sick, and I regretted going myself ever since. It was a terrible experience with them pushing cocaine on me, and then making me feel bad if I refused. It was a set-up from the start and it happened just before the poisoning. I agreed to meet them at the bar but they never showed. While waiting for them, and trying to figure out what happened, I was accosted by two men, threatening to rape and kill me. The one with a knife took a swing at me, but with the adrenaline rapidly rushing through me, I hadn't noticed that he had actually sliced me across the stomach. I was so pissed off that I managed to kick the bastard in his thigh with my stilettos before turning to the other and kneeing him as hard as I could in his groin. They both hit the ground groaning, and I was able to escape back to my car and get home. It was then that I noticed the blood trickling out from under my ripped black silk shirt.

When I got home Tom had a look on his face that told me he had something to do with the attack. He must have been livid finding that his plan had failed, and the reason he was so relentless with the poisoning attempt. I knew one thing; worse evil people than Tom had tried to kill me in my lifetime, and failed.

Tom would have to get a lot better at this if he was going to succeed, because he sucked at it.

Now Chloe was at my door so I didn't know what to expect. She hugged me softly, sympathizing about our breakup, and trying too hard to convince me she was my friend. I really didn't trust her, thinking that Tom might also be responsible for her visit, and his next attempt on my life. I was cordial, but on guard while we sat and had a glass of wine together. The boys were still at the pool, and I could watch them from the front window. Again, to my surprise, Chloe got up and closed the drapes, before pulling a baggie of cocaine out of her purse. She separated it into two lines, pushing them toward me. I hadn't done any drugs since the night I was attacked, but I took it just the same, asking myself why.

I had been controlled over the past 30 years; punished for not doing what I was told, and then married Tom who made my life miserable if I didn't comply to his demands or what he asked of me. The alternative to taking the coke was to fall asleep from the many hours of sleepless nights, building my business. After I snorted the coke, it was like her phone rang on cue, and she quickly got up and said that she had to go, leaving the other line for me to do later. She left with a distant hug, and an apology, knowing I would never see her again.

I hurried to put the other line of coke away so the

boys wouldn't find it, and as I sat there starting to feel the effects of the drug, I got this enormous amount of energy and many ideas for my business. I went to the dinner table to quickly write them down before opening the drapes again to make sure the boys were okay. After they went to bed, I was up the entire night again, working and accomplishing more than I could imagine. I was focused and alert with these new ideas to grow my business bigger and better, and I was quite impressed with myself for being capable of doing such good work.

In the morning, the boys woke up to find me still working at the table and asked if I was up another night without sleep. I casually told them that I had gotten up early to finish some work I had to get done. I made their breakfast, got them off to school, and then headed to the florist for my deliveries.

By lunchtime, I had finished work and had lots of cash in my pocket. To say I was exhausted was an understatement, but I headed home to do the leftover line of coke in my bedroom and then get back for more business ideas. I tried to resist the temptation, knowing I would be awake again another night, but my resistance was too low, and as I snorted the line, I could feel it taking over my mind and body again.

The boys came home after school and did their homework watching me work again at the dinner table, and noticing the change in my appearance. I had lost even more weight and was looking pretty shabby. When they mentioned it to me, I just smiled and told them I was fine and not to worry. They went to bed like good boys without a problem, and as predicted, I was up again the entire night.

Another week quickly passed and it was their father's turn to take them for the weekend. I looked forward to those weekends just to relax, but he always seemed to weasel out of it, saying he had another business trip to go on. The boys would beg me not to make them go each time because they claimed it was hell staying with him for the entire two days. I didn't want to stir the waters in my so-called relationship with Tom, so I made them go, hoping it wouldn't be the biggest mistake I could make.

The weekend quickly came and went, but apparently, this time, Tom didn't drop them off at the door, and the kids walked in alone, telling me that they had walked home themselves from their dad's apartment. He had tried keeping where he lived a secret, but I knew he was living in the same complex close to the eighteenth hole of the complexes golf course. According to the kids, he had just moved to a two-bedroom apartment, closer to us, so the red flags were weighing heavier on my mind with what he was up to next. I was trying to hide the growing anxiety inside, remembering the fraudulent insurance policy and poison, and now thinking he was going to try to take the kids away from me, or worse, another attempt on my life

We had been at our apartment now for a few months. Tom's behavior toward me had gotten worse with so much contempt, likely because of the $1,500 per month his lawyer instructed him to pay me after our separation. Knowing how cheap he was and how precious his money meant to him, I started getting worried at what he had up his sleeve next and it wasn't looking good for me.

Once the house sold, Tom gave me a small amount from the sale, but with no proof of what he actually received for it, I never knew how badly I got he screwed. It was supposed to be half of what the total payment was, but with the little he gave me, I highly doubted it. With my share of the money, I wanted to put a down payment on a nice little house for me and the boys, but due to my US status, and our recent divorce, it required a co-signer for the mortgage. I banked the money trying to find the nerve to ask Tom for his help co-signing, but when I did, he flat out refused, with no explanation, whatsoever. When I got back into my car, something inside me just snapped. This was the last straw. I was tired of everything I had to fight for in life; physically, mentally, and emotionally.

CHAPTER 36

It was the start of the summer vacation at school, and without the break I badly needed, I decided to send the kids to Canada to spend the summer with my parents. Both mom and dad were so happy about seeing their grandchildren, and with them both being boys, I knew that my dad would love the father-son things they could do together. I called Tom for him to make the arrangements and pay for the trip, and I wasn't surprised when he agreed. This just meant he didn't have to make excuses for not taking the kids on his assigned weekends for the next two months.

I took them to the airport. They would be supervised during the trip until my parents picked them up at the airport. I would get the much-needed break to grow my business and try to relax without any interaction with their dad.

Little did I realize that my children's absence would be the catalyst of what was to become of me? My cocaine habit gradually increased as my business grew. At the same time, so did my connection with the seedy dealers I found to help me feed my habit.

I would soon discover that these dealers were such uncivilized torturous monsters that I never knew could possibly exist, and I would be the one responsible for sending them to prison for the senseless murders of their many victims. The path of hell that was about to be laid out before me was something I should have seen coming, it would take a miracle to defend myself against, and there was nothing to protect me here in a country where I didn't belong.

How I had gotten in so deep and so fast was surprisingly easy. It was the damned drugs, and I blamed my husband for most of it. Growing up, I had been given drugs by my family doctor for pain and diet purposes, then, forced consumption by the monsters that attacked and raped me, and eventually the little I did of my own volition, but it was never out of control like it was becoming now. It wasn't so easy to quit, and soon, I would understand why. In the meantime, my entire life was falling apart before me, and once again, I found myself trying to stay alive.

The only difference between the life I knew growing up and what was about to happen here, was that the criminals emerged from both sides of the law. These cops were more dangerous and much worse than the murderous animals they chased. They had more at stake than those they fought against, and the means to hide it better with all their training, or they would just simply kill whoever got in their way. Their criminal acts were nearly flawless but in some way they were involved with those they hunted; and mysteriously never charged for any of their heinous crimes. That was baffling to me, and being who I was with my childhood experience, I needed to figure it out. Why, I wasn't sure.

I was just thankful that my children were gone for the summer, which meant I had two months to dig myself out of this perpetual cesspool of hell I was being dragged into by the most sinister monsters from both sides of the law. I couldn't think how it could possibly get worse until I found myself forced to live *"Among the Guilty, Under Attack."* (book 2)

Printed in the United States
by Baker & Taylor Publisher Services